ROCKETS ON A ROPE

The Legend of the Great White Groom

Britt Darby

Editing and Book Design by David Thrasher
Cover Design by Steven Ross

First Edition

ISBN-13: 978-1503329546
ISBN-10: 1503329542

Uncle Chuck's Farm

My first experience with horses began with my uncle Chuck, who had a small hobby farm south of Des Moines, Iowa, the town where I was born. He was a tall gentle man, a gym coach who had been a professional basketball player in the 50's. "Back when whites played Pro ball," he would say. Married to my mothers sister, he picked me up after school every couple of weeks to help him with the chores. I was ten at the time. Finally big enough to pitch hay.

Frosty was a dirty white horse with huge feet and a back that sank from years of saddles. My uncle would lead me on him around the barnyard as I dreamed of being a cowboy in the far off west...without him leading me.

I remember being intrigued by the rare visit from Ol' Doc Ron, the local vet, who drove an old Ford pickup with a box full of curious contraptions. Doc would treat a barb wire fence wound with some magical remedy he carried in his overall pockets.

Rockets on a Rope

I grew up by a shopping mall in the suburbs, surrounded by what seemed like a zillion miles of cornfields with Interstate running through it.

My mom was an Avon lady who baked us cookies for a living, took me to church, and potato salad Christian parties with relatives. My Dad was and is a Boy Scout through and through - Trustworthy, Loyal, Helpful, Friendly, Courteous, Kind, Obedient, Cheerful, Thrifty, Brave, Clean and Reverent. He lives by and exemplifies the Scout Oath: "Be Prepared."

As an only child (my brother and sister had gone off to college years before), I was a brilliant young guitar player fully absorbed with the indoor pursuit of fame and fortune.

Waiting for my uncle I twitched excitedly, watching the second hand on the classroom clock, knowing he'd be pulling up in his bright red truck at exactly 3:10, sometimes with it loaded twenty bales high with hay.

By the time I was in high school the trips had stopped and I had developed into an awfully talented singer and performer, winning countless talent shows, playing Beatles and Monkees tunes. Upon graduation, I met another gifted young genius and we formed the musical duo "Britt Darby & Brett Young". We were good, not just "Yeah, sure you sound great when you're drunk" good. We were really good...possibly and probably great.

After nine months playing in the "Seventies" atmosphere of the Iowa bar scene, we met a Dr. Berglund at a resort area in northern Iowa called Lake Okoboji. He and his kids had been coming to see us regularly and liked the Crosby Stills and Nash songs we played. Dr. Berglund had invented the soft contact lens. He offered to fly us out to San Diego to play in the parking lot at his company party...which ended up being 300 Vietnamese worker bees who just happened to know the words to every Dan Fogelberg song. Dr. Berglund was a generous genius.

We packed up and moved to La Jolla, a cliff lined, beautiful coastal village just north of San Diego. We started working the assembly line at Berglund's place until we got ourselves booked into the California club circuit, which we played for a year. This included a place called the Winners Circle in Del Mar, by the horse racetrack. Just like the gigs in Iowa, we soon discovered the bars in California still had some drunk guy in the back yelling, "Play some Willie Nelson!" About that exact time I developed nodes on my vocal chords and started spitting blood onto a microphone. This was not hip in those days. I was told it was caused by many years of doing spot on imitations of all my favorite singers, from Julie Andrews to Frank Zappa.

Brett returned to Iowa, because I was going to need a year of not talking to rest my chords and rehabilitate. My parents had flown out and taken me to the Scripps Institute, conveniently located in La Jolla. There we met an aging opera doctor, Maurice Schiff, who had seen my MRI and told me, "Do not take your Rolls Royce to a Chevy repair shop." He had retired from practice but would work on my case as he could see I was a serious singer.

While relaxing in La Jolla, I was not to speak for six months. I would carry a note pad with basic things written in it like, "Hi. How are you? I can't talk." and I would learn to write out my thoughts. Dr. Schiff would eventually perform a delicate surgery that a Japanese film crew shot footage of. This had put a slight twist in my takeover of Hollywood. Needless to say, I loved that summer of crawling over the Cove on the beaches and going to daily therapy to regain my voice.

When “Britt & Brett” had played back in Des Moines at a Howard Johnson’s lounge out by the Interstate during the 1980 election campaign, a man came up to us in the middle of a song and told us to “Keep playing” as they ushered out our audience and escorted in the whole Kennedy herd. I don’t think all of them were 18. I know uncle Teddy wasn’t. He was funny as hell and running for president.

Anyway, it turned out they too, like the Vietnamese, liked Dan Fogelberg and Crosby Stills & Nash tunes. Brett played solo Neil Young songs until four in the morning and I ended up talking with, and getting to know, John F. Kennedy Jr.

One night in La Jolla, a year and a half later I guess, I was cruising along the rocks and saw John, sitting by himself out on a cliff. I walked up quietly wanting to say hello but instead flashed my note pad. He laughed, “What’s up with that rock star?” I held up the page that briefly explained my predicament. "Seriously, dude you’re a good singer, that's too bad, whatever.”

“Hey let’s go get something to drink,” he offered. We strolled up through La Jolla Cove Park to the liquor store. If you’ve ever been there you know it’s beautiful - the cove, I mean.

As we left the store we saw a wild looking, homeless sea captain standing by the garbage cans out behind a sushi restaurant. The back door swung open and he was handed a white package containing three salmon steaks that were too old to be served. He turned around to the two of us and asked, “You scallywags starving?”

"Sure," John said.

"You got any money?" the old pirate begged.

"Oh, don't ruin it for us," John pleaded.

Pointing to the liquor store, the old fart ordered, "Go in there my scallywags and buy the best champagne and we'll drink it while I'm cooking dinner."

We ran back in for more brew and followed him down to the cliffs above the Pacific, where he had hidden a small grill and a bag of charcoal. John had bought a really expensive bottle and after a few drinks, I still remember the old guy looking at the label, kind of funny. It wasn't Boones Farm. The grilled salmon was superb. The old guy was oblivious.

When we got up to leave, the old man said, "What are you two sailors named? I forgot to ask?"

"Britt," my friend replied, "and I'm John Kennedy."

"We all are, you drunk son of a bitch. We all are," the old guy informed us.

I ran into John a few more times. Once in a Beverly Hills underground dance club at 3 a.m. he seemed . . . kind of wired. He said he'd walked into a K-mart that day and saw 50 TVs showing his dad getting his head blown off. He was getting tired of that. We all are.

Eventually I did get my voice back and I got a blind date with some girl in Hollywood whose dad claimed to be in the biz. She drove me all around pointing out the sites.

Rockets on a Rope

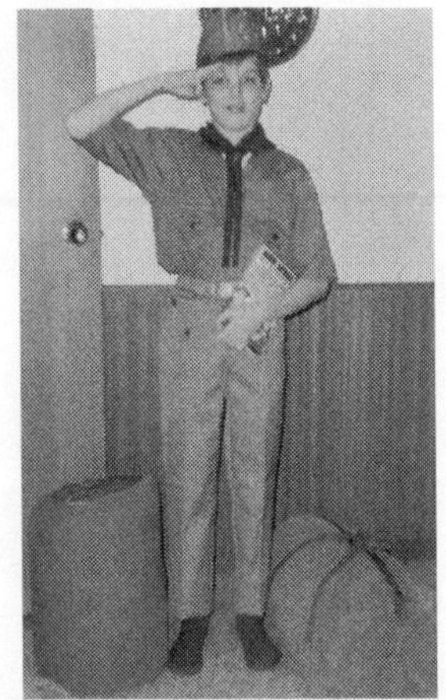

As a Boy Scout, always "prepared"

My first "guitar"

Britt & Brett in Des Moines

Britt & Brett in Hollywood
Henry Diltz photo

Hollywood 1981
J. Parti photo

Santa Fe 1996
Willian Coupon photo

Uncle Chuck's Farm

Thousands of homeless movie stars, garbage in the streets, hookers and traffic congestion. There was small adobe recording studio next to a big church, in a complex called Crossroads of the World, with palm trees and a fountain. It was Graham Nash's Rudy Records, a private studio for Crosby Stills & Nash and friends.

I was approached while I was loitering there by a wiry long haired little man named J. Parti, who smoked a cigarette in the courtyard that smelled like Ethiopia. He was an engineer working on mixes of the Eagles' *Live* album. With flaming red-eyes, he inquired if I "had a license?"

I said, "You mean a backstage pass?"

"No," he said handing me a fifty dollar bill and pointing down Sunset Boulevard.

"Go quick to the Highland Liquor and get Glenn a bottle of Absolute Vodka."

I went as fast as possible. I returned and tapped on the darkened windows of the studio entrance. Showing the bag of goodies, I was allowed in and offered a seat in the control room which was out of control. Other wired looking people wandered in and out for the next few hours. One was Glenn Frey, the self appointed Big Bird of the bunch, and shorter than I'd imagined.

About 3 a.m., as everyone wandered away, the burnt out engineer turned around, extending his hand. "J. Parti," he said again, "How long you been working for the Eagles?" "Uh... Not long," I stated. I started to explain my trip up from San Diego when he said, "Shh shhh ssshhh, Ok, ok. You can stay here tonight. Just clean up the whole place in the morning and have coffee ready by ten." He locked the studio door behind him and there I was . . . for the next three years.

That morning, after I'd vacuumed up a bunch of white dust off the black piano, Mr. Graham Nash showed up. Without saying much, he handed me the keys to his Mercedes and asked me to go pick up his sons, Jackson and Willie, from a friends house. No questions asked.
And so I began my internship with Crosby, Stills & Nash. Brett came back from Iowa, moved in with the secretary, helped answer the phone, and rolled packs of cigarettes. I cleaned the studio every morning, ran errands and was the food guy for the '83 Crosby, Stills & Nash *Daylight Again* Tour rehearsals, loading my Cadillac trunk every morning with $400 worth of sandwich stuff and a case of every kind of beer for the band and the crew.

One of the only memories I have of that experience was when Mike Finnigan, the keyboard player, nodded at me to bring him a shot of whiskey just as they started playing *Carry On*. I carried the glass up the stairs on to the stage. I walked through the three singers, gave Mike his drink and, when I turned around to leave, I realized I was standing in the middle of Crosby, Stills and Nash. And they were a mess and they sounded completely out of tune.

One interesting adventure was driving a rented tow truck in the middle of the night across the Mojave desert to retrieve world renowned session bass player George "Chocolate" Perry, whose car had broke down. I was told to get there ASAP and ask the first huge black guy I saw at four in the morning at a Motel 6 in Yuma, Arizona if he was "Chocolate?" That was exhilarating.

Uncle Chuck's Farm

We ended up meeting and being around most of our childhood idols and musical influences. We grew up fast. On days when the studio was empty, we wrote and recorded a lot of original, smart tunes.

I spent my free time scouring the streets of Beverly Hills. One afternoon I ran into Cher who was shopping on Rodeo Drive. She liked my hair and set up a meeting for me with her A&R man at CBS records, producer David Kahne. He and Norman Winters, a big time publicist for the likes of Michael Jackson and Elton John, really liked our music. But he could never find the right commercial angle to push it past "The Gate Keepers". Our music was creative and unique. It didn't fit the corporate mold.

Berglund had blown a wad of cash on a 45 rpm single we made at Rudy Records the week CDs came out. My Dad had spent $30,000 he didn't have on a recording we'd done in Des Moines called *New Age Waltz*. We were now under contract with an investment group called Miracle Entertainment and not real happy about it.

Anyway this book is about horses, So we're gonna get to that real soon, promise.

It was the 80's and, after years of getting frighteningly good at finger picking and singing like angels, we were suddenly trying to compete with the L.A. New Wave and Hair Metal movements. Crosby, Stills & Nash and the people around them were going through some sort of a rock star mid-life crisis and weren't necessarily the people we needed to meet when we first got to town. It gave us a nasty attitude to begin with and I was unimpressed and disappointed with everything and everybody by the time I was 25.

Rockets on a Rope

The 1985 recording of our grand finale was called *Inisosion*, a word and concept we spent quite a good deal of time and energy on, as well as a good deal of the investors money. It was kind of an existentialist “Pop” opera. It was probably not the smooth commercial move to make during the minimalist Punk scene. We had put all our proverbial eggs in one basket in our pursuit of a "major label deal”, unaware of the fact the system was itself failing. We actually never had a Plan B and now too many people were telling us what we should sound like when we had always just sounded like ourselves.

Brett and I weren’t centered. Britt Darby & Brett Young went down in a fiery plane crash, into a bathtub in France.

One night Norm Winters invited me to the CBS Christmas party where I started talking to somebody’s daughter. She said she really liked our music but the bulk of our conversation was about a National Horse Show that was going on at the Burbank Stables for the next two weeks. She told me we should check it out. So we did. I loved it. The smell of the horses in the smoggy atmosphere reminded me of Uncle Chuck’s farm. The Mexicans scurrying about with carts of hay and the other sights reminded me of Frosty.

I spent the night sleeping in my car at the show. The next morning was exhilarating. It woke me up. Unhappy with the direction the recording money was taking us, I took my guitar, a microphone, and my amp and rolled onto the elevator at CBS Records, Century Towers. I was heading for the office of David Kahne, to play a new song called *I Wanna Live Life Like Jesus*. An older fellow, who smelled of Vodka and was totally wired, was already inside. I assumed he was a janitor or something.

He asked me what I was doing. I told him, "The clowns running this company would not know a good song if they heard it and I'm gonna show David we're the best thing going and Tommy Mattola and Walter Yetnikoff (the CEO's) are idiots! And Springsteen sucks!" I was pretty proud of myself.

Anyway David liked the song. He actually liked most all our stuff but it didn't matter anymore because the guy on the elevator was Dr. Walter Yetnikoff. And it was Norman's daughter who had taken me to the Horse Show. She'd left me there, going off with her own friends, but apparently hadn't come home for a few days. David and Norman were not happy and that was the end of my enthusiasm for Hollywood.

That afternoon I called Tom Tucker, who had engineered our *New Age Waltz* project in Des Moines in '81. He was now running Prince's Paisley Park studios in Minnesota. He invited me back to meet the Artist, though I really had no interest in him or his music. I drove back to Minneapolis to see what might happen and here's what did: As Tom introduced me to Prince, I shook his hand and said, "My friends have a German Shepherd named Prince."

That afternoon, because I had nothing better to do, I answered an ad in the Minneapolis paper that read, "Wanted: Barn worker for sixty horse dressage stable. Live on, will train."

Brightonwood

As I arrived that next morning I was greeted by Kathy, the owner and trainer of a sixty horse dressage training and boarding facility, located in the quintessential tiny town of Maple Plain, in the rolling hills and lakes outside Minneapolis. With my shoulder length hair and Hollywood attire, I told her of my horse experience to date: Frosty and the intriguing show in Burbank. Right then the phone in the barn office rang. "Hold on a minute," she said, lifting a finger in the air as she ran off to answer the call.

I leaned up against the nearest stall door. It was of a dark horse who stood with his butt to me and his nose in the back corner. "Howdy, what's up Trigger?" I swaggered egotistically. He turned and drug his lazy feet through the deep wood shavings towards me. He hung his apparently depressed head over the door, sort of pushing me out of the way - nicely though. I brushed his mane out of his eyes and stroked my hand along the side of his massive cheek bone. This wasn't Frosty.

Rockets on a Rope

Kathy came back down the sacred passage with a stern, serious, almost inner reflection, kind of stare.

"You're hired," she said never smiling, not really showing any indication of emotion at all.

"Really?" I declared, not really sure that I wanted to do it. I was not entirely sure why I'd driven out in the first place but was pretty damned sure it would give me an idea for a song.

I stood there listening to her explain what the job required. I pretended to pay no attention to the horse behind me nuzzling and blowing through my hair. I got a spiritual like feeling that I wanted and needed this job. So I decided to ignore him completely. I just acted like there wasn't a huge animal nibbling on the nape of my neck like my mom and dads schnauzer, Patches, used to do back home.

Kathy explained in further detail, there was a bunkhouse apartment on the backside of the barn no one had lived in for years. I was welcome to clean it and move in that day. Suddenly she was handing me the keys to the huge diesel farm truck twenty minutes after we met and sending me off to the Maple Plain Tack and Feed Store. As the truck lurched forward she screamed out, "And get a cat too! Not a kitten! A Cat."

After I loaded up the plastic buckets of Bute, Biotin, Source, and mineral oil - horse stuff I supposed, I decided to drive over to the local Shop & Save. I picked up some pinstriped overalls like Uncle Chuck used to wear, a camouflage baseball hat with a picture of a deer getting shot, and some heavy duty rubber "muckers" boots I'd been told I'd "be needing." I also grabbed one flannel shirt, some long underwear and ten pairs of wool socks. Premonition, I suppose. I thought I'd better look the part. "When in Rome," as they say. Driving back I saw a combination thrift store/animal shelter, so I pulled in and picked up a "Banjo".

As I forced open the bunk house door, a hundred mice scampered into a hundred holes in walls held together by cobwebs. It smelled like my uncle's whole farm in a pleasing kind of way.

"Its not much," she stated, "but you're not paying rent" which was a new idea to me and a novel concept that I assured her was better than Beverly Hills in a lot of ways.

Banjo and I stayed up pretty late that night killing things and generally scrubbing the whole place down with Clorox bleach which my mother had assured me "would kill anything." Morning came quickly as I awoke to the sound of a tractor starting up. Sixty hungry horses were beckoning and kicking at their stall doors. I watched a figure, appearing almost like a Ninja warrior, run through the cold morning air into the barn. I threw on my new duds and hurried down to the barn. The cat was chewing on a mouse on my kitchenette counter. I left the front door open.

I was met by Ariana, a short Japanese woman, who looked at my attire which looking back now I concede kind of made me look like the guy from *Wayne's World.*

"Hi I'm Britt Darby," I declared.

"Great," she sighed, wiping her nose with an icy coat sleeve as she turned and started trotting quickly down the aisle toward the grain room where I had strategically placed the buckets of supplements the day before.

Brightonwood

"She only hired you because Max likes you."

She sounded unhappy.

"Who's Max?" I inquired.

"That big stallion at the end of the aisle."

"Yeah, She was sweet," I haphazardly offered.

"It's not a 'she', you asshole! It's a stallion."

"Oh yeah, well... I wouldn't know the difference."

"Great!" she moaned.

Ariana proceeded to advise me that he was a Hanoverian, direct from Germany. Kathy had recently acquired him and no one in the place had really gotten any kind of control of his aggressive manner. He was "a piece of work," she sighed.

She rolled out a carnival hot dog vendor's cart and saw the merchandise I had gotten. "Wow, when did this arrive?" She smiled.

"I did it yesterday," I said proudly.

"Cool," she purred. "Come on."

Then we proceeded down the single aisle. Twenty nine geldings were on the west side, thirty mares on the east. I was instructed to read the stall card and deliver grain in exact amounts with supplements and vitamins to each captive.

"The vitamins are under here!"

As we went down the line, she explained the different substances, purpose and why it was given to each specific horse. The reasons included sore and achy bones and muscles, mane and coat growth, and "attitude adjustment." That sounded pleasant. There was also a posted amount of either alfalfa or the lush timothy grass to use, or a combination of both. Usually about two flakes per horse, three times a day. Most horses will toss it out of new fangled feeders. Its better for them to eat it off the ground anyway, like grazing naturally.

As we finished breakfast she ordered, "Go get the tractor. I started it for you already. You do know how to drive a tractor properly?" she suggested, sounding a bit like the camp marshal in *Bridge Over the River Kwai.*

"Uuhh, sure," I hesitated, remembering hanging on to the fender rumble seat on Chuck's ol' John Deere.

"Great," she surrendered. "I'll go with you."

She proceeded to "properly" instruct me as to the steering, brakes and "propulsion". Then she gracefully demonstrated how to use the two hydraulic levers to load up wood shavings in the front end loader. She also explained how to attach a diabolical contraption/trailer known as a Manure Spreader. Oddly enough, Brett and I had done a radio jingle for a manufacturer of such, in a far gone galaxy. I drove the assembly into the barn aisle, which was just barely wide enough to pull into, and shut the barn door behind me.

Ariana predicted, "Here's your Future Fork," as she handed me a modern, aerodynamically designed, high-tech horse shit heaver. I spun it in my hand like a baton.

"Don't destroy it," she scolded. "It will be your business partner for the next four hours."

(Charming.)

Before we began to clean most of the horses were to be turned out, nineteen geldings to the west, fifteen mares to the east, into lush green pastures .

Ten would go out to solitary runs and fifteen would remain inside for boarders who arrived periodically through the day and evenings. When I asked why the boys and girls were segregated, seeing how there was only one stallion, she gleefully and proudly responded, "The mares would kick the boys asses." She laughed. After being shown how to properly place a lead rope and halter, we escorted the groups out one at a time, although I would gradually learn to handle two or three at a time.

I returned to find Ariana standing by Max's stall with his halter and a three foot silver chain attached to the leather lead rope.

"Ok, Hollywood," she proclaimed. "Let's see you take him out."

To the farthest enclosure, of course.

"And come back alive."

Quaint.

"And if you don't return, it's been a pleasure working with you."

She explained further.

Rockets on a Rope

"When he gets all over you - crank down like this." She motioned like some riverboat captain blowing his own horn - A lot!

"You can't hurt him. He can kill you - and he knows it." It was definitely not the same guy from the snuggle session the previous day. He was pacing back and forth at the gate to his kingdom, screaming in a louder, huskier voice than the others. He was blowing and snorting from side to side, like he was late for something.

He hardly moved out of the doorway as I slid in. Placing the halter over his bobbing head proved more frustrating than with the others, some of whom bowed their obedient noses through the nylon steering device. I did get it on and loaded the chain in the proper manner. and we proceeded into the wild blue yonder.

He immediately shoved his shoulder into me as we trotted forward kind of sideways. I pushed back into him with my shoulders and hips with all my weight as we zig-zagged out the barn door, prancing down the path to his playpen. I was pretty much out of my comfort zone as we were now outside and he was pushing and pulling me. Still, in a weird Siamese Twin like way, he was staying with me, working with me. I got more confidant quickly and focused on our destination.

I closed and locked the gate, a maneuver I would learn was an "Automatic Must" according to my boss. As I released the setup over his nose he exploded - all four feet off the ground. It scared the holy hell out of me but was exhilarating at the same time.

He danced and raced around the enclosure frantically bucking and kicking up a cloud of black dirt dust. But I would peek out to check on him in about a half hour and he would be standing like that old painting with the drunk Indian on a sleeping horse. When I returned, hanging the rope on his stall door, I smiled like I had just conquered Attila the Hun. Ariana made no comment until she said, "Ok, get to work", pointing to my trusty plastic sidekick waiting by the first stall.

She didn't show me how to do it so I assumed it wasn't that hard. So I dug in, literally. We didn't use carts. You'd just carry each load to the door and toss it in the trailer and then move on. I started to leave my first stall until I saw Ariana was still in hers. So I went back in and kind of stirred the wood chips around a bit, as I waited until she had moved on. She asked, "Are you getting the pee spots?"

"Uhh yeah, sure," I replied.

"You must get the pee spots."

I picked a little better at door number two.

When I arrived at #9 she was three or four stalls ahead of me. Her steeds must have pooped less I assumed. My arms, wrists, back, and legs were beginning to feel the labor, which was quite different than playing my guitar. By the time my task was fulfilled to completion, Ariana had been off riding her horse "Zen" for quite a while. As I stood there heaving, she yelled from the indoor riding arena, "Take the tractor straight out a half a mile or so and flip on the slot machine lever on the side. Then drive around in circles until the thing is empty. Unhook it and put the tractor away, then start filling water buckets."

Which, at this point in the day, were already forming ice on the water that remained.

I shivered in my soaking wet sweatshirts as I slowly looped around the sprawling hillside. I could swear I heard the theme song to the old TV show Green Acres playing in the background. I did the dinner feeding by myself and crawled home for the evening. And we slept.

The cat was tired too, despite the gnawing and patter of the last of the occupying army throughout the remaining walls. I was tired as hell. I had very rarely mowed the lawn back home because my dad liked to do it. I really had spent a good deal of my life singing with a guitar in my hands.

The weather report on the six o'clock news had warned that a major winter storm was blowing into the area and I fell asleep way earlier than I ever had in my life. Next morning the radio alarm clock cheerfully notified me there was sixteen inches of snow and it was a balmy twenty-two below zero. Banjo was chewing on a mouse on my kitchenette counter again.

I left the door open and headed out into the arctic environment. The tractor cranked hard but it finally creaked to life and, as I dropped the metal hitch-pin into to 3⁄4 inch hole, an unfamiliar ping sounded in the bitter air. Lord! Even the apple chariot was frozen. I slid the heavy, ice caked, barn door open to enter as the pungent odor of ammonia bit thru the morning air.

As I began feeding chores it seemed as though the stink was coming primarily from my side. Ariana didn't arrive until after I had watered, using a hammer I carried in my overalls to dislodge the frozen barrier on top the water.

Brightonwood

As she approached she inhaled an all encompassing, chest heaving breath and smiled happily, mentioning, “Nice job on the stalls.”

“Thank you,” I accepted.

“This is not acceptable,” she retorted. "You will have to strip yours down to the rubber mat,” she explained. “I have other commitments today, so I shall unfortunately have to leave you in command. Also, you will have to complete my stalls.”

My body throbbed.

“And the horses don’t go out either.”

I wondered why?

“You’ve got all day. So get to it.”

Now a horse stall is usually, hopefully, 12 x 12 feet and a horse is roughly 1200 to 1600 lbs. - if they're friendly. The task that had seemed relatively easy the day before now seemed increasingly daunting.

“And don’t give them carrots,” she added as she left. “Carrots are rewards, not treats and not to be provided as bribes.” Well I didn’t have a carrot, but I looked around for a guard standing watch over me. I’d probably eat them myself, if I had any.

The first stall wasn’t too bad. The sleepy pony sighed, farted, and moseyed around me, like we were doing some waltz she had done everyday her whole life. I had abandoned my trusty Future Fork for a square edged shovel Ariana had thoughtfully provided. I began to sweat under all of my clothing. The barn door slid open and in walked a very tall wiry cowpoke, a very dirty, strong man named Skip. He was a ferrier, a horse shoer by trade.

He walked up and shouted, "Hey, green horn. Where's Ariana?" I explained she had "appointments elsewhere" as he inhaled, like he was smoking a cigar, and quipped, "Somebody missed their pee spots." I thanked him for the astute observation.

He said he was there for the day to change the shoes on as many of the fifteen as he could get to. Working horses have their shoes changed about every six weeks according to hoof growth and wear. "Are all the sons o' bitches in?" he asked.

"Yeah," I said, already sounding tired. "Well, I'll help you out if I can."

He slid the next stall door open and took the horse out for a fitting.

He and I worked in silence for the next few hours, except for the inconsistent flaring of a gas forge and the pounding of a hammer, interrupted by a sharp "Stop it now. Quit, quit."

"Stand up straight, you asshole." I stood up straight as my back burned. Just to be a swell guy, he not only moved the horses he needed but he rotated the remaining ones around. So I pretty much had the working room I needed. I got done amazingly faster than expected. I completed throwing one last shovel of shavings in and shut the door, just in time to see Gem the dapple gray inside drop a new pile of steaming green gold, and she looked at me and sighed and grunted like she enjoyed it.

Brightonwood

Finally finished, I slid the snow encrusted door open and was greeted by an icy dagger plunging through my damp clothes. The daily commute to the pasture was a torture. I steered the tractor with my elbows as I clinched my gloves in prayer, hunched over the wheel. When I returned, icicles had formed on my eyelashes and on my chin where I was growing a beard for the first time, or at least not shaving. I came in shaking off the cold like a frozen dog.

There was a wealthy looking woman in her 60s who had arrived and was standing beside Skip and a dashing white inmate.

"Are you the new boy?"

Mrs. Steele politely offered a leather gloved hand.

"What do you think of him?"

Looking at the horse, who I'd hardly noticed before, I said, "Oh, he's Grand."

Skip looked up at me and slightly shook his head.

"Lovely," she proclaimed and elegantly retreated to the tack room.

Ariana came back, looking into each stall as she said "better" to no one in particular. "Hey asshole," she cooed as she stroked the great white horse's mane. They seemed to know one another. Skip struggled slightly with the impatient patient. "Quit, quit," he hissed, dropping the hoof, breathing a well deserved sigh. He glanced at the horse sharply and under his exhausted breath said, "Asshole."

He handed the lead rope to me and asked if I'd put him away.

"Gladly."

As I took him in, he slammed me against the entrance of his sanctuary.

"Asshole," I delightfully responded, when I heard a woman's voice behind me say, "Remington, Son."

"His name is Remington Steele." she explained.

I turned to see the patron standing like a soldier, with a whip under her arm.

"Yes sir, I mean Madame."

In reality I only knew a few of their names. Max. I knew Max. As she led Remington away, I recalled how I'd only heard him referred to as "Asshole" and he seemed to respond to it. Remington was actually pretty inconvenient when you were yelling at him. I wondered if they knew their names.

As I finished up water chores Ariana walked up with a stern, serious, almost inner reflection kind of look and said, "Good job today."

I stared back dumbfounded.

"Tomorrow I shall teach you to muck properly. You will never muck, improperly again! Ever!"

Brightonwood

I wearily struggled through the snow drifts back to my shack. I felt as though I'd just been drafted into the Kamikaze Pilots Association. The next morning she did show me how and I'm not going to explain any further other than to suggest; if you do it properly daily and do it right consistently, it gets easier and faster. The secret was, I would learn, that it was less a part of the job and more something you just had to do before you got on with the job. Really kind of a Zen thing, if you approach it that way.

One nasty 22 below morning Ariana asked me to take all sixty frozen ice and hay filled water buckets out into the sun in the front parking lot, clean them, and then return and refill them. Halfway through my chore a boarder, who rarely visited, walked straight past me and, upon arrival at her stall, yelled out, "My horse has no water!" I smiled, sort of, and responded, "I'll get right on that."

Spring approached and the grasses of the open pastures beckoned. The horses started going back out. I had survived the winter and gotten very efficient at my task. I didn't really dawdle much with the individual horses as I was more a part of the herd. Ariana did that very properly. The boarders liked me and I eagerly did my job.

One particular sunny afternoon, as I went out to call the crazies in for dinner, I saw one of them slip on the slow drying Minnesota mud, taking a rather dramatic spill onto his front shoulder. He slid a few feet, then regained his balance and quickly rejoined the galloping group. Entering the paddock area, the whole group veered off single file through a single open gate. They stampeded into the parking area and beyond.

Rockets on a Rope

I remembered a movie I'd seen where Sonny, this drunken rodeo cowpoke, sets this huge black million-dollar racehorse free in the desert.

As I stood there, watching my life pass before me, Ariana laughed robustly and motioned, "Make sure all the stalls are open and the gates closed."
"They'll be back, they've got nowhere else to go," she assured me.

I warily obeyed and sure enough, one by one, ye verily, two by two, they sauntered back into their own stalls. I slid the cell doors tight behind them.

"Damned jail breakers," I said. "That'll cost you carrots."

It was pretty hilarious. My mentor scolded me.

"Always check your gates. Walk out backwards. Always be secure in knowing you have done the job properly. and through to completion."

A few days later I was told there would be a woman arriving who was a world renowned Equine Psychic. She was a homeopathic soothsayer as well as a massage therapist and healer. I wondered what she could do for my back and arms and for how much? She went from horse to horse, gliding both hands, with crystals tied to her wrists, along their legs and backs.

She came up to Kathy and stated that the little bay gelding Sasha had told her that he had fallen down in the field a few days back and had a sore shoulder. It truly was the horse who had fallen and risen up again. I had seen him fall. I knew them all by now and their distinct personalities.

I didn't say a thing to anyone but as I walked past Remington's stall I smiled, nodded knowingly. and greeted him, "Hello, Asshole."

One rainy morning in mid March, while climbing over one of the white wood picket fences, I crashed down onto my right shoulder. The pain was intense, a solid burning deep inside my neck and arm. I had broken my collar bone. Ariana felt my arm like the voodoo lady. She told me a doctor wouldn't or couldn't offer much help. "Do you have insurance?" Of course not. "Well go wrap yourself up and stick a wet finger in the Bute bottle. But don't do it often. It'll rot your liver." My liver was already on its way to rotten, so I put on a clean t-shirt, duct taped my aching shoulder into a workable position and went back to work.

I understood the philosophy of mucking now. I successfully suffered through a couple weeks. As everyone knew I was a hard worker they cut me some slack. Even the horses. Sunrise in April I awoke to the sound of a Minnesota mosquito knocking on the front door. I'm not kidding and if I have to explain that to you, you've obviously never been to Minnesota.

I had learned much, grasshopper! And I found I not only loved horses but they loved me. I even liked Ariana in a respectful sort of way. I told Kathy of my plan to go. She said she was sorry to see me leave but knew I needed a break. I was physically worn out, yet at the same time, mentally stimulated by my little vacation.

I assumed it was probably time to return to Lost Angeles and see if anybody missed me. That afternoon Mrs. Steele arrived, handed me twenty dollars, and asked, "Where will you be heading, son?"

I said I'd been thinking about driving back to LA, down through Santa Fe, New Mexico, a place I'd driven past a number of times on holiday trips back home. She told me of a delightful dude ranch where she and her husband had visited just last summer.

I slammed the trunk of my car down and turned to see all of them standing there in the parking lot. I saluted, then hugged Ariana. I shook Mrs. Steel's leather glove as she delightfully replied, "So long, asshole." I turned and thanked Kathy as she handed me an embossed Brightonwood envelope.

"That's a letter of recommendation from me", she pointed out. "You can pretty much go anywhere in the world there are rich white women, show them that, and they'll hire you."

I still have that letter today in my box of treasured things, like a college degree. As I drove out the long driveway, I saw Max standing, staring right at me, perfectly still. I slowed down, then stopped, looking at him for a minute. He snorted. Then I spun the wheel to the right, turned the radio up loud, and stepped on the gas pedal, heading off towards the great Southwest to the haunting rhythm of the Eagles' *Hotel California*.

The Santa Fe Trail

As I came down the Raton Pass into northern New Mexico, I turned right into Cimarron, the famous town on the famous trail. I drove past Philmont Scout Ranch where my father had taken countless Boy Scouts from Iowa to enlighten them that the rest of the planet wasn't a cornfield. I made my way around the stunning Enchanted Circle that leads to legendary Taos, then south down to Santa Fe.

Eight miles north of town I saw a sign with an arrow pointing to Rancho Encantado, the place Mrs. Steele had spoken of. Walking into the dude ranch headquarters, I handed my letter to a woman named Ronnie. Her mother, Betty Egan, had owned and operated the place forever.

I stood at attention like some pony express rider who had come from a far off battle. She read the note and said, "You want to start right now?" grimly pointing to a large pen, a ravine really, with thirty dude ponies who stood silent in a sloppy bog that, in the name of the King of Spain, I shall call "The Urine River."

Rockets on a Rope

I was introduced to the troop. Connie was the head wrangler, a pistol packing cowgirl from New Hampshire. Bonnie was the suntanned señorita, whose husband painted all those really weird portraits of Michael Jackson. She ran the boarding barn. Then last, but not least, Lonnie, the other ranch hand I'd be swapping stories with. I would be called "Scrawny."

Ronnie...No, Connie...No, Bonnie led me up the pathway to the boarding barn, which was actually a football field sized tin shed. It had a red tin roof and forty privately owned horses with no stalls, per say - just a row of fifty foot individual runs protected from the gorgeous southwestern skies.

The first horse she introduced me to was Rising Star, a small unassuming bay that she told me had been in the movie The Electric Horseman. Stabled next to him was a buckskin named Buck. I was told the owner, Bob, would call every so often and ask to have the two horses saddled and tied at the hitching post by the main lodge. There would also be an older Indian man named Ralph who would ride on a more regular basis. I decided to not worry about specific names since I'd just gotten done memorizing sixty at Brightonwood.

I finished up the "indoor" mucking quickly. It was easy - no shavings, no actual stalls. So I slopped my way into the pig pen, dragging a cart up to Lonnie who was standing calf deep in a murky mix of yellow-green foam, sand, and mud. He was short, stout, hung over, and a kind of worn out looking man who didn't say much and was evidently not interested in my story. He'd stop and stare off into the distance, then return to scooping shovels full of crap into the cart, which he'd then drag off to a sandy arroyo. Finally we stopped fishing and Lonnie allowed me to do the evening chow line. He sat in his truck, slamming down a six pack before he drove off into the oncoming sunset. I waved to Ronnie and told her I'd be back at sunrise as I drove off to nowhere in particular.

I headed down into the village of Tesuque, nestled in the Sangre de Christo foothills, north of Santa Fe Plaza. Driving slowly through the gorgeous valley, I spied an incredible place with a large Hacienda and a pretty large guesthouse close by, with white picket fences like Kentucky, only in New Mexico. I backed up and drove onto the magnificent estate which had a little wear and tear not visible from the Bishops Lodge Road. I drove down the cottonwood lined drive to an area in the back, next to a huge grass pasture. There was an old pickup with legs hanging out of it parked next to what looked to be a funky multi-colored tack room shack converted into a clubhouse fort kind of a deal with a toilet and a sink.

Pat jumped out of the cab like he hadn't been sleeping for days and rubbed his face and eyes. I offered him two hundred a month for the place and said I'd help out with his horses when I could. He said he didn't need any help. He did it all himself, including taking care of his ailing mother in a wheelchair, but he said he'd take the money. So, just like my invitation from J. Parti in LA, I moved on in for what would be three years. I crashed out on the floor, tired from the just now ending drive from Minnesota.

The next day I showed up completely amazed by the desert mountain splendor of just my commute. Upon arriving, I was told by Connie that Lonnie had shot himself last night after work. She offered no explanation, but asked if I'd be willing to have a go at it by myself eight days a week, no vacation. So, since I had nothing else to do, I volunteered.

And ended up doing it non-stop, 7 days a week, for the next full year.

That morning I noticed a big red horse named Redmond who had been laying down when I arrived and didn't get up when I fed him. He kept chewing on his stomach, acting as though he was going to roll over and die. This caught my attention so I called the owner, Kit, to ask if this was his normal mode of operation. It wasn't. "Oh god! No! Colic!" she cried. "Call Stuart. He's my vet. I'll be there as soon as I can."

They both arrived about the same time and at the same place. Kit was wearing a thin white halter top underwear t-shirt (it was a cool 50 degrees that day) and clean brown riding breeches with Armani knee-high stomping boots.

Stuart looked like a younger, more romantic version of the Marlboro Man with his new white Stetson hat, crisp white ranch shirt and stethoscope. He had a charming white smile that actually seemed to sparkle like a toothpaste commercial. This was not ol' doc Ron. This was the cutest vet in the west. He approached the unhealthy animal, whom I'd gotten up and was leading around in small circles. "Looks kinda uncomfortable, don't he?" He checked his heart rate, respiration, and pushed his thumb into the horses upper gum and watched the white spot slowly return to pink/red. He also knelt down and took a pulse from just above the hoof. He pulled a syringe from his pocket and proceeded to diagnose the situation.

"I'll give him this shot of Banamine to relax him. Kit and I will run over to the Rancho enchilada cantina to have a margarita while it takes effect."

They walked off, arm in arm, chatting about the weather. It took effect pretty quickly and I wondered if they had a chewable tablet. I thought that would be kind of a cool name for a horse. Banamine... high ho and away!" Stuart appeared to have a pretty neat job.

When they returned, he brought with him a six foot yellow clear rubber hose, a bucket with a mixture of mineral oil and warm water, and a large syringe hand pump. He quietly asked me to "hold the horse" with the lead rope in my left hand and my other hand holding the blaze on his upper nose bone.
"Now don't let him go."

He slid the oily tube up the horses nose until there was only a foot or so remaining in his hand. Then he used the pump to send the warm mixture to the stomach. The tired horse squirmed in front of me. He pulled a three foot rubber surgical glove from his coat and proceeded to move his arm slowly, carefully, as far as possible. up the rear end of the startled patient. (Yes, he certainly had an interesting job.) Proceeding to pull out massive globs of dry looking manure, he tossed it down on the ground.

"Well, call me back later if you see him looking goofy again or anything suspicious."

He hugged Kit and then drove off to save some other damsel in distress' horse,

After a while Ralph, the Indian of the Ralph & Bob Show, showed up, saddled Rising Star and rode off into the hills. Interesting enough Bob arrived a couple minutes later and inquired as to where his horse was. I looked at him and sarcastically stated, "I let him loose".

"What?" the bewildered man asked.

"We took him out and set him free. Didn't you see the movie?"

Mr. Redford shot back a glance like the Sundance Kid then slowly calmed down as I explained that Ralph had gone out only a little while before.

"Ya want I should saddle up Buck, horse whisperer?"

"No, no," he said. "I'll just clean some stuff up in my tack trunk." He walked away kind of smiling, kind of wondering who the hell I was.

I finished sweeping the aisle. Ralph finished his short ride. Redford had finished up his tack box chores. Bob walked over extending his hand, holding a pair of hand-held wire clippers. I looked at them supposing they'd probably be handy for trimming new guitar strings or cutting hay bale wires. He asked, "You got any use for these?"

I said, "Thanks a lot", never wanting to turn away a free gift from a living legend. I slid them in my right front pants pocket. They remain there today, twenty-five years later.

I saw Bob again not too long ago. He told me Rising Star had died a few years back at age twenty-nine. "He was a great little horse," he said looking at the ground. "Movie Magic."

Now there were some other entertaining events that summer. Of the notable occurrences, there was the time Connie came riding in fast, all out a breath, saying, "Saddle up. We got ten scared-stiff New Yorkers rambling about god knows where all." A child's birthday balloon had floated by on the trail like a tumble weed spooking the horses every which way, distributing dudes all over the place. We had us a tourist round-up.

Then there was the time I loaned a semi-clean sweater on a chilly morning to a gal from California. She had forgotten to give it back prompting her loving husband, who'd hopefully had too many margaritas, to show up at feeding time accusing me of having an affair with her. I calmly explained I was really busy and had dated fashion models he'd looked at in magazines and didn't have the slightest interest in his fat, unattractive middle class wife.
"Alas, she held no allure for me."

I patted him on the back as he sat in the dirt crying and apologizing to himself. I told him perhaps the fiesta was a good time to rekindle the fire for them and gave him directions, away from me, to Zozobra, a celebration in the plaza next summer.

"Over there," I said, pointing west, away from the barn, away from me.

One fine day, a short, thin Latino cruised into the barn with a stocking cap pulled over his eyes and a tattoo on his neck. He asked if "Ronnie was around?" like a dope dealer. I said, "No, but the job had been filled" by me and " we didn't need any help." He shot back a stare that looked just like the underwear model on the side of that skyscraper in New York. It was he, Antonio Sabatical, Jr. Yeah, so as it turned out, it was the guy on the side of the building and he had a horse there named Pancho.

He asked if I knew of a trailer he could borrow and a place to board temporarily. I suggested the Beasleys. He had heard it from high up that Boss Betty was sick. The place had been sold to some corporation and they were gonna unload the horses and put in a golf course or a high-end health spa. The ride was over.

That afternoon, as I finished up dinner feeding, Ralph showed up. He had taught roping and riding to the *Young Gun* clowns and *Silverado* cowboys, to name just a few films shot here in New Mexico. He informed me of an Italian western TV series going into production on the old west sets south of town. It was called *Lucky Luke* starring Terrence Hill, the blonde haired blue-eyed Italian star of the *My name is Nobody* and *Trinity* spaghetti westerns from the 70's.

Ralph asked if I'd "mind trying out" for being an Indian extra, or an extra Indian. He mentioned that half the guys applying couldn't really ride that well and didn't have long hair. Since I had long hair I'd be fine. "Here." He threw me a girth with a handle on it and stirrups, but no saddle, and gave me a colorful Indian riding pad. He said, "Put that on the calmest looking horse you see right when you first get there."

"You'll be perfect, marvelous," he deadpanned.

To my surprise I got the part of white buffalo boy and as the ranch closed down for renovation I excitedly pondered my new career.

Tesuque

The first day on the set I stood around in my stirrups under the blanket while the others sat uncomfortably on their mounts. Vanya, a Yugoslavian assistant director, walked up and announced, "Guys, guys...Yes, people. Attention please?" he begged in broken English. "I have never worked with horses...or Indians before," he said to the solemn stares of the tribe.

It was kind of a low budget operation which I didn't notice because we ate all day and spent a lot of our time sitting or standing around in a line for lunch, or on some hill overlooking the fake western town. Mimicking an impending attack of Geronimo's warriors, we actually never really moved, except to eat. It was a comedy and that was one of the gags. Not much actual riding, which was good because I really hadn't ridden horses that much, ever, and I was eating more than I had in awhile. The long twelve hour days were tiring enough, just doing nothing.

One 3 a.m. morning, waiting for a sunrise shot, we were standing in line like Sitting Bull and his band. An older sage pulled out a bag of a magic mushroom/peyote blend and handed it to the next brave in line. It was thoughtful of him to have brought enough to share with everyone. The sun psychedelically crept up into the red, yellow, and purple haze. We sat tall on our painted ponies with bells, feathers, war paint and all. I don't have the slightest idea how to describe what I was feeling and I cannot and will not explain, except to say our Vision was interrupted by a shout, "Nice shot. Beautiful, guys. That's a wrap."......Lunch!

Over the next ten years I would be a bit player in *Gun Smoke* (actually with James Arnez and Ali), *Wyatt Earp* (Costner's version), *The Wild Wild West* (sucked), *The Lazarus Man*, *Did You hear about the Morgans?* (probably not), *Due Date*, and *Thor*. All were filmed on one of three movie sets on the south side of town, all with delectable dining and a 12 hour atmosphere.

I didn't necessarily learn that much about horses other than:

(A) They don't like explosions or gunfire half as much as people do.

(B) When the director told you to saunter down the dusty windy street, pull up to the saloon, get off and go in, as the excruciating takes wore on, you could gradually slow down a bit each time to where you weren't having to get on and off and on all day long.

"Back to One...Lunch!"

One very windy day a large group of us were to ride up to a creaky saloon in town. The dust and the spooked horses were a handful. Lunch was...dusty. The next day we had to do a pick-up shot of the same scene, only the wind wasn't blowing. They brought out aircraft engine fans...seriously. We came whipping around the corner and everybody went every direction. The horses loved that. The director didn't.

About the time *Lucky Luke* was winding down my car decided to die. But I really didn't need it anymore. Walking up and down the postcard picture perfect Bishops Lodge Road through the heart of Tesuque was flat out inspiring. I hardly ever needed to go to the big city. I began to pick up small private barns here and there in the multitude of million-dollar mansions scattered through the historical hamlet. Apparently Forbes 500 named it on a list of the most beautiful places to overpopulate. It was literally littered with celebrities: Redford, Hackman, Danson, Oprah for Christ's sake,... James Taylor, Elliot Porter, Dylan, Winger, Roger Miller, Terrence Hill, Val Kilmer, The Dalai Lama, and Ali MacGraw, the babe from the *Love Story* saga who every 14 year-old boy in the audience fell in love with in 1970. I was 10.

One particularly nasty winter's eve, walking back from the village market in my now work worn cavalry brown cowboy hat and my dad's 1947 Navy submarine overcoat, a voice lilted under the clouds above and behind me, inviting.

"Son, can you step in here a moment."

Grace opened the door into a cozy front room with a fireplace, lined with trophies, medals, photos and bronze statues of figures that appeared to be throwing horseshoes.

"What's yer name, boy?"

The bellowing voice came from a big gray man, sitting backwards on a kitchen chair, fiddling with threading some leather stitch work of some intricate bridle ornament in his well worn hands.

"Britt" I quipped.

As he looked at his wife with a broad smile like that of a fourteen year-old boy, he said, "You look just like a fella I made Calvary saddles with over in North Africa during Doublya, Doublya Two. The hat, the coat, the hair... He was a Brit. What's your surname?"

I said, "Darby."

He asked, "Like the Irish Derby?"

"English," I replied.

Slim in his shop

Tesuque

Well it turned out Slim was a saddle maker by trade and knew just about everybody and their brother in Tesuque, with horses and visa-versa. So I didn't have to look for work any longer.
One day I stopped to gaze in at his spectacular work shop, adjacent to a small loafing shed with his one horse, Bard. I walked in, ringing a set of shiny spurs which hung on the door knob. He was measuring actor Robert Wagner's ass. I pulled up a bench and admired the amazing museum quality display of bridle bits hanging on his ceiling - flat ones, straight ones, curved and twisted barbwire artifacts.

Wagner didn't notice me nor I him but I pondered whether my first question should've been "What's the only kind of wood that doesn't float?" Instead I asked the grand wizard, "If a horse is salivating a lot and leaves a wad of unchewed hay in the dirt under him, what's going on?" Wagner turned to me and nodded.

"He needs his teeth worked on. Whose horse is it?" Slim inquired.

"Ola," I said, "from Debra's Rancho Piano."

I passed through the property everyday to feed and muck her three Peruvian Paso's and Ola, an Arabian parade horse who'd dealt with shriner midgets. Bombproof. I rode him a lot in the evenings.

"Well go fetch him while I wrap this up. You can step down now, sir." He gestured to the mannequin.

I trotted the spunky, dusty old fart down into Slim's classroom barn. Oh, did I forget to mention his name? I don't like to be a name dropper. He was Austin "Slim" Green, one of the finest saddle makers in the wild wild west, and the rest of the world for that matter. He'd come to New Mexico from Oklahoma by Wagon Train in 1911 and was instrumental in forming the Santa Fe Rodeo. His saddles sold for upwards of $7,000 to the likes of Roy Rogers, Gene Autry, Tex Ritter, Ronald Reagan and Randy Travis ... and the 7th Calvary Regiment in World War II.

As he carried out a bucket of files to greet us. He told me some Japanese documentary film crew was coming by "pronto tonto" to shoot some footage of Slim at work. "I told the sons a bitches they were welcome if they got down on their knees and performed 'harry-carry' for me!"

Apparently they had agreed or surrendered because right then a Mercedes van with about thirteen little kamikazes inside pulled up. They spilled out in a line carrying cameras and excitedly bowing as they removed lens covers.

"Do you think they brought enough of 'em?" Slim pondered. "Probably not."

"Now most of what has been discovered, observed, known to be true and proven about horses," he began, "was figured out by the Romans as they attempted to cross the Swiss Alps on their way to invading Siberia or somewheres."

He handed me the lead rope, pried open the beast's teeth and began to file away like a self-trained dentist on the outside molars. He'd file then stop and squint into the horses mouth, then start filing like a madman again. "You getting all this, Fujiami?"

"Shoes, bits, medicines, cures," he called them. "They basically had to figure out what worked best, or else lose their horses and their war."

I would eventually see this procedure done with a cross between a hand held chainsaw and a jackhammer, like they fix the streets with.
He went on to proclaim: “None of this bullshit they’re coming up with now is any better. Most the time it’s idiotically worse. Automatic waterers, hats and coats, youth-in-Asia. Lord! They die faster when you shoot ‘em in the brain. Jesus Christ!”

He preached, “The horse has survived for 25 million years without us and what have we done for them? Besides using them to win wars, build railroads and settle the west?

(Sort of.)

“You think these gooks speak English? Lets take a break, girls,” he decided as he threw the file back in the bucket and continued explaining. “Ya see, these pointy little burrs form on the back teeth - calcium in the water or what not and end up tearing the inside of the cheek making it hard for them to eat. That’s where a lot of ‘ribby’ horses come from.

"You gotta pay attention to what the horse tells you. Don’t ask him to do something. Let him believe it’s his idea. Make him wanna do it with you. You get in a tug of war with Man o’ War, you’re gonna lose. And there is no such thing as a free horse.”

He stopped.

“Hey! Anybody here got some Saki? Bueno, comprende? Kawasaki, Nagasaki?”

He was a one of a kind, multi-dimensional, beautiful man. Probably one of the nicest afternoons I had was the day

Rockets on a Rope

Slim handed me a hand tooled leather wallet. He said he made it for me in a "couple-a-minutes" while he was waiting for some "yay-who" who went by the name of "Franz Klammer." Val Kilmer, I presumed.

Now I'd heard all about Mr. Kilmer and his reputation, or lack thereof, from Pat. Because "Mephisto", which suits him better, had rented the large guesthouse on the Beasley's property three years before I arrived, he had just made it big in Top Gun or something. I didn't know of it. I didn't have a TV.

Now he was getting involved in some Oliver Stone production about Jim Morrison and the Doors and getting his ass measured at Slims. He barely noticed me when I told him I was living at Pats, but when I said my name he did notice me. He said a friend of mine, Dad, who drove Bob Dylan's tour bus and had listened to a lot of my music, had mentioned something about me being "pretty wild, especially liquored up - and I had a nasty attitude but a voice like silk." And could imitate just about everybody.

Val offered me $250 a day to help him tear down some old fences, put up some six foot tall pens for some buffalo he was getting, and clean out the horse barn on the recently purchased property. We'd work together like buddies as he lost weight for the part. (Apparently one of his many issues.)

We'd listen to the Doors over and over and over as I'd consume as many beer/whisky, boilermakers as I could in a twenty-four hour period while he observed me like some kind of a crash test dummy. Was he serious? I pleaded, "Yeah" as he pointed out that he didn't quite have the part yet. Stone had been advised that Val was a professional jerk. But he was gonna buy a wig, make an audition video, learn

"how to be Morrison" and take it to Stone, who would not be able to decline. Sounded like a plan.
I had rarely drank or done any drugs growing up in Mayberry but the Crosby, Stills & Nash experience had introduced me to a new way of looking at things and I was rather good at it...Looking at things. Val also assured me I would probably be his double, stand in, and stunt runt. For in the past it had seemed most directors chose not to use him when they didn't have to. Now the way I saw it, I had other things to do that day, so I told Kilmer I'd try and get through his security gate "manana."
Saying "Adios" to Slim, I headed over to Roger Miller's place. Yeah... That Roger Miller, the King of the Road.

I walked up the Nashville crooner's long driveway, where I saw "Rusty", his one horse, standing in the field with a magpie on his back, like a rhino in North Africa. I normally just moved a few stacks of poop in his modest corral corner every so often, not on any regular basis, as Roger's fort was pretty far off the beaten path and Rusty did a lot of his job in the beautiful pasture where he lived. Alone.

Roger had a really cool tire swing. It sailed over the Acequia that surrounded his house, possibly one of the sweetest spots in the Valley. As I raked my future fork, properly spreading the dusty dust smooth, Roger wandered over and said, "What's up?" Then he asked if I could "possibly come by twice a day, check on things, and feed and water Ol' Rustwagon" for the next two weeks while they went out of town to accept some award.

"Yeah... I guess I can." I hesitated since I was walking and it was kind of a long way to go for five bucks. "No Problem." He pointed to a car parked by the barn under a dirt brown cover.

"You can use Old Blue."

As I drove the '76 Rolls Royce Silver Shadow up the drive to Val's castle the next morning, I thought to myself this was a pretty ideal set up. I figured all I had to do was pull up to the Tesuque Village market in the classic car, run into Ali Macgraw, sweep her off her feet and everything would be just peachy. I did end up sweeping off her front porch and parking cars for a party.

With actor Jack Elam on the set of *Lucky Luke* (1992)

On location with the cast and crew of *Lucky Luke* (1992)

Movie Stars... Swimming Pools...

Val tried to act like he didn't notice the car as I got out. He noticed the car. I could never tell if Val was acting - or acting like he was acting. He was actually more of a mimic from the Juilliard School of Mime. He'd also gotten his saddle before his horse - in almost every aspect of his life.

We started moving unpacked junk around the cluttered new stables and I thought I heard in the background what sounded like "Woke up this smorning and ah' got mysaillf a beeear." Actually I did. It was blaring from the balcony of his Villa repeatedly, over and over and over, for days at a time.

Now today we were going to bury a dead buffalo that had been delivered in the back of a beat up trailer with Pecos plates. Some country vet had shot the beast something like 13 or 18 times since he "hadn't ever tranquilized a buffalo" and couldn't predict what it would take to bring the great cow down. ("The white man?" I suggested.) Anyway it stank to high heaven as buzzards circled and encroaching coyotes howled and yipped it up as though they'd found Eldorado.

Rockets on a Rope

We ripped through his phone lines with a back hoe as we dug a swimming pool sized tomb. Pat Beasley had come up with a Vietnam vet shaman to sing an ancient Indian burial chant, which spoke something along the lines of "We're sorry, Mr. Buffalo." We threw in hay and water before placing the animal facing west to the sunset. The next morning Val stopped by to inform me that two other buffalo had mystically appeared at the site apparently smelling their brother from their pens 5 miles away. They had broken out and shown up here. Val ended up adopting them. Too bad for the buffalo. Now that afternoon I needed to drop over to Elliot Porter's place and rake the fall leaves, as I was still holding on to all my other chores because I had no reason to trust Val, and for good reason. When I left that day, I asked how much he wanted to cough up for a good horse? He responded, "Oh...six thousand or so."

The old man sat in his front picture window in a wheelchair and I'd wave as I raked up the different colored leaves that he had made a lifetime career taking photographs of. Eliot had pioneered color film with the likes of Eastman and Ansel Adams. His son Patrick asked if I could go help him muck out his overdue corrals. When we went in through the gate he shushed away a big ol' clompy brown horse that looked as though it was from the movie Willow. Shaking his old metal pitch fork, Pat yelled, "Yeehah! Get on out of my way, you six-hundred dollar piece of shit." A light bulb burst in my head. Did I already tell you I was a genius? I was.

"Hey that B-picture clown who just moved up the hill said he was looking for a horse for around six thousand bucks. You should call him up. Here's the number."

I saw a flash in Pat's eyes like Pat Garrett. Val really was in a flick where he'd played Billy the kid. I went home that afternoon with five-hundred dollars cash in Slim's wallet. I now had a new feather in my cap, "Horse Trader" and oh what a fine exchange it would be.

Later on down the road, Val would take my new girlfriend Kate back to L.A. with him which eventually led to his divorce from the Black Queen in Willow. What was her name?

In return for showing him how to sing well completely inebriated, he never acknowledged me publicly or paid me a lot of the money he had promised. And he ended up dropping Kate off in L.A. after about a week.

I did run into Val once more, unfortunately for him and his dad, who was visiting and looked a lot like Orson Welles when he was senile and fat. We were up for one more round all around as I sat at the bar in a local watering hole that had been an 1800's stagecoach stop and whore house which had been called "El Nido."

As the two stood waiting for the Maitre D, I whistled and patted my hands on my thighs impatiently. "Here Val. Come here, boy," whistle, whistle, pat, pat, pat, "Come on Val," as the dining room fell silent.

He walked over like he thought he was Doc Holiday.

"Yeah...What?" he challenged.

"Well I just wanted to thank you for taking Kate off my hands. That was mighty kind of you."

"What business is it of yours?" He pleaded insanity.

Rockets on a Rope

"Well, I just thought I needed to tell you I've got AIDS."

The greasy hair on his fat head stood straight up just like the iceman he was. He flew out of the stunned, hushed restaurant! and I have never seen him again. Praise Allah. I was politely asked to never return to El Nido, forever.

Once, to my delight, while sitting on the front porch of the Market with Ola, a busload of Texas cheerleaders drove up and I gave them Val's gate entry pass access, his phone number, and a map to the star's home, etc, etc. I'm sure he appreciated it. I did. They did.

I'm very happy for him, as he's progressed from bad-ass to fat-ass, and I'm sure he'll be thrilled with my depiction of him, as any publicity is good publicity. And just to add a little fuel to that fire:

Once when pulling up to the mailbox on the road at the Beasleys, Val got a fan letter from some 11 year-old kid from Ohio, in a wheelchair no less.
The kid had sent a self-addressed envelope and a dollar, asking for an autographed photo. (God knows why?) Val slipped the dollar in his shirt pocket and tossed the crumpled letter out the car window. I'm not lying. I believe he was trying to be cool. He wasn't and isn't. He is an insecure, insincere, Christian...mimic.

Well it was my time to leave the Beasley place too. Pat informed me that he wasn't too thrilled with the shoot-out at the Not Ok Corral. Rents in the area were skyrocketing and he could get a lot more than the token I was offering.

His older brother Pete, who was losing his eyesight and was also the current Mayordomo of the Acequia Madre which irrigated the lush desert hideaway, wanted to move in to be closer to his mother, Winnie. She was the stuff of New Mexican folklore and the matriarch of the three boys - Pete, Pat, and Dennis. Brought up in military school by a single mother who had secretly flown bomber missions in WWII without orders, "The boys" were then set loose on the monumental Tesuque plantation, ripe with ancient Indian ruins, to enjoy a rootin' tootin', high falootin' life that made them a cross between the James Gang and the 3 Stooges.

I learned many things from Pat. He was a Renaissance man. My time spent there was a series of late night pool games and daily drills about horsemanship. I hated to go but I wasn't going far. Half a mile down the Bishops Trail was the forty acre estate of Debra Dant, called Rancho Piano. I scouted out a cute little beat up Silverstream camper from behind an art glass blowing shop and moved it over to the place.

Debra let me park my trailer way out back by her three Peruvian Pasos, Flamo, Rose, and Pandora, and my adopted companion, Ola, who I eventually rode into the Village Market one night to get some beer and True cigarettes. I got kicked out for life...Off and on.

The corrals and sheds were actually situated alongside an embankment of trees by the cemetery and a 400 year-old church. The Acequia ran by the front door. It was an irrigation canal, dug out in the 1100's by the Anasazi Indians and given as an offering to the Conquistadors.

The first night I was tucked into my new palace the most intense thunder and lightening storm I had ever been in rocked my campsite and I wondered if I would float away down the vanishing, then reappearing in torrents, Arroyos. The second evening I heard the mournful melody of an old Spanish requiem being strummed softly by four old men with three guitars and a fiddle, “Adios, Adios, Adios.” They sang as they buried another descendent of the conquerors who came 400 years before.

The Spanish were something new for me to enjoy. One day, as I spoke to my mother on the pay phone outside the market, a Harley-Davidson chopper rumbled the concrete as it pulled directly up to me, riding it a major vato in a headband with tattoos and scars and stuff, and a badger ugly dog, a blue heeler, riding and standing on the vibrating gas tank.

“Get off the phone!” he ordered, walking at me menacingly.

“Hold on Mom. What?”

“Get off the phone!”

I pointed to my left and right and suggested there were two others available.

He said, “I want this one!”

I said to my silent parent, “I gotta go, Mom. There’s some Mexican biker dude who’s needing the phone, so I gotta go.”

“Thank you,” he smiled in the Spanish tone I have grown to love and admire.

"I’m not a Mexican biker guy,” he said like a valley girl.

“I’m a Spanish, motorcycle enthusiast.”

I walked inside the market quickly, grabbing some beer and approaching the counter. The phone rang. Sharon, the cashier, answered. "Yeah? Hold on," she said, handing me the receiver. "It's for you."

"Hey friend. It's me. Andreas. Outside. Remember? With my little dog, Monkey? Hey, can you pick me up a half pint of Dark Eyes Vodka por' favor', buddy?"

Sharon had already retrieved the loot and was adding it on to my bill. As she hung up the phone, she said, "He does this all the time to tourists" and laughed.

Actually living in Tesuque was a bit like living in the middle of somebody else's vacation. "Don't worry he's a snuggle-bunny. I promise," she said, and I quote.

As I handed him the cheap bottle of Vodka, he slapped me with a closed fist on the back of my still sore shoulder and the grotesque puppy wagged its mangled tail like a golden retriever. "Cool brother," he said, kicking the explosion that was his ride. And they rode off. I called my parents back and didn't say a thing about what had just happened. I wasn't sure myself and wished someone would explain it to me.

To make a long story very short, I will only say, that besides learning all the bad words in Spanish from him, I cried like a baby the day the Santa Fe Police, the Sheriffs Department, the Highway Patrol. and Tribal Police, all stood in a straight line, saluting. Andy was good at what he was.

His ashes were thrown into the wind with a thousand colored balloons in the church parking lot where his Harley sat silent with Monkey sleeping by its side. He was 40. I was 40 when he died. "Adios, adios, adios," Amigo. To which he would have responded, “Eee, I’m not really your amigo, but you've got a friend.”

There was always something new and different to attend to. One winter day I got a call from James Taylor who informed me there was a small herd of wild burros which his wife Kathryn had “saved” from the Bureau of Land Management. They had eaten every last shrub in the small enclosed acreage they were in. These rascals were free when they had been bought.

I explained, “That’s what wild burros do for a living. They eat everything in sight, like goats, only bigger and way more intelligent.”

“We’ve been feeding them,” he argued.

“Well, in a group this big there are going to be more dominant ones that’ll gobble everything right up,” I said. “leaving little for the others. Get it?”

“Maybe,” he said, surveying the barren pinon trees scattered about.

“You got too many,” I suggested.

He asked if I might possibly find some other generous souls who might provide homes for these wayward vagabonds.

So I did, spreading the six orphans throughout the valley. J.T. kept two (smart idea) and Debra and I got one. We named him “Burrito”. I put him in with Ola and the girls and slept well that night knowing I had contributed to the saving of a sacred life. Perhaps Burrito’s ancestors had helped De Vargas take over the New World or stood by the manger and pulled straw out from under the baby Jesus. Who knows?

Movie Stars... Swimming Pools...

The next morning, when my trailer door slammed open, Burrito let out a loooooong (wind-it-up baby), excruciating, horrifically loud, hilarious bellow, announcing to the universe he was hungry, like an echo in some far off canyon in Utah, where they were free like Rising Star. The other five joined in a mournful chorus. It felt like we were in the Ozark Mountains of Missouri, not Bethlehem. Stuart Ashman, the director of the State Foundation for the Arts, took the other three. He dresses up like a hillbilly and gives little children burro rides in the De Vargas Parade that goes by the De Vargas Mall on De Vargas Street every summer Fiesta. Nice life, if you can get it.

I'm not sure Sweet Baby James got it. That spring he called to see if I could babysit a stray dog they had taken in before they left for New York the next day. So I went up and found this fat old black lab running up, wagging her tail, like she was glad to see me as I yelled, "Bella go home!" pointing over to the Leinberger's place next door. James walks up as I ask, "Where's the critter you want me to feed?" He gestured to the overweight glutton waddling back to her own million-dollar home.

"That's the neighbors dog, rock star!"

"Yeah, but we were feeding her and she acted like she was starving."

Aaarrrgghh!

"The French poodle that won the Westminster Dog Show would eat out of a garbage can if you gave it one! Please don't adopt any more strays!" I said as I walked away from ten bucks a day for six months.

Rockets on a Rope

One last quick superstar story:

Mr. Summer decided he wanted to learn how to tie a diamond hitch pack mule knot and drag his innocent donkey up into the Santa Fe National Forest, which butted up against his property. I got a marine Iraq war vet friend of mine, Kevin, to come up one glorious morning for the lesson. As he tied his first knot, the finger picking champion of Martha's vineyard broke a finger nail on his right hand. Looking up at his wife, he said, "What do I do, Kitty? I got a show to do next week."

She showed him the way back to the house for some clippers. Kevin looked at me and said, "I like some of his songs and all, but I'm not signing off on Ziggy Stardust taking this burro on a backpacking adventure. Period. It wouldn't be fair to the burro."

We informed the adventurer of the change in plans. He stared blankly, kind of like Ziggy Stardust - at the end of the trail. He came over to the house once to hear some of my original compositions. He called them "Quirky." Never quite understood what he meant.

At this point I was still working on my music, playing by myself at a place called the Cowgirl Hall of Fame. Two articles were written about me in the Santa Fe newspapers and I was still writing and recording quite a number of songs with various other musicians, including bass player Kenny Pasarelli who had played with Joe Walsh, Elton John and my lyrical hero Dan Fogelberg, who I met one day at the Tesuque market with his wife Anastasia. Kenny told Dan that I could do a spot on imitation of him and I informed him how it hadn't helped me out much in L..A. and had pretty much left Brett and I behind the times as to what was "hip." He didn't appear to like me. The last of my disappearing idols...

Among other notable musicians in the valley was a pathetic, yet still egotistical, Kip Winger. He was a serious musician who had been squeezed into make up and spandex tights by his record label and into the hair metal band "Winger", a band which went down in history as the image on t-shirts only the losers on the Beavis & Butt-Head Show wore. He was considering working with me until l suggested he'd have to wear one of those shirts. Allergies forced him to Nashville to pursue a career in classical music?

I also met and had lunch with Jon Densmore of the Doors, who I met at the Market and discussed the idea of forming a band with Noel Redding, Jimi Hendrix's bass player, who was now actually living in the tack room I'd been in at the Beasleys. Noel, unfortunately, died before we got a chance to do it. He was pretty much broke and involved in a lawsuit with the Hendrix estate. And my desire for the music business dwindled.

Which was fine because I really was enjoying the horses and the colorful assortment of employers I had collected. One artistic moment I was needed to escort Veryl Goodnight's horse into her home/studio for her to sculpt. As I held the sagging rope, I looked at books about her grandfather Charles, pioneer of the famous Goodnight Trail. Then there was the archeological time when I surfaced ancient pottery shards and human relics while I was properly raking the dust in the Lienberger's stables. Apparently it was built on an Indian burial ground.

I worked a month or so for an Arabian breeder, Sally Rogers. Her horse, Barexi, had been the Arabian World Champion many years earlier and had graced the book cover of *Vavra's Horses of the Sun* but was retired now. He had his 10-foot long tail all wrapped up in a bundle, beating against his back legs all day. It was pretty sad. For all the attention and glamor he'd had in the past, the Arabian hay day had passed and he was just a dusty old horse now.

Sally's Mexican had had some trouble sneaking back across the border, so I was filling in for him. Sally was in the middle of a divorce from her husband, Max Coll, who'd been elected to the New Mexico Statehouse, both as a Republican and a Democrat, and he was the chairman of the powerful Budget Committee.

One day Max asked if I wouldn't mind taking a truckload of manure from a 20 year pile over to the new place where he was living with his new girlfriend. As I was loading the pickup with the beautifully aged compost, Sally stormed out and asked what I was doing. When I told her it was going to Max, she screamed, "You tell that son of a bitch that's my pile of shit!" His reaction when I informed him of her decision...was neutral. I loved the fact that he had an undocumented worker too.

One night Debra gave me a walkie-talkie and sent me over to Oprah's house, a half a mile away, to adjust a patio spotlight that was shining into Debra's bedroom. She directed me over the receiver, "Down a little bit, over, over, no the other way." A large black servant came out from behind a curtain and demanded I leave the premises.

"There are people inside here, who can't be bothered."

I said to him, "Relax Giles. My billionaire's bigger than your millionaire. Over and out."

They ended up putting barbwire fencing around the whole place, cutting off centuries old riding trails. Ola' and I ran into it at a trot one day in an arroyo we'd been up a hundred times. I flew over his head and I walked him home with his chest covered in blood. We survived. He was bombproof.

Probably my crescendo and apparently my grand finale were the three German tourist girls who I met in the plaza and invited out for a ride. They stayed with me in my little trailer for three weeks to the delight of Carl, the UPS guy of the rich and famous. He honked his horn every time he'd see us riding about on the horses with Burrito running along beside. But all that was about to change.

The Ballad of the Mayor Domo

Within two weeks of just getting rested up after Claudia, Berlin, and Katrina, I met a waitress at the Orehouse Café on the plaza one night. Realizing that the one time with the three was possibly enough, I invited Melissa out for an afternoon ride the next day with Ola and Pandora... Pandora indeed.

I was now working a lot for Terrence Hill, the spaghetti western hero, who had purchased an old farmhouse on the river that had originally started out as a chicken coop the old Spanish folk told me. One day, after a pretty hard monsoon, he called to ask why the place "smelled like chickens?" I went over and ripped up a window sill where the smell seemed to be strongest. We discovered feathers and bird crap and chicken wire covered up, kind of, by a crafty real estate agent's putty knife. I said to Nobody, "Looks like you bought yourself a million dollar chicken coop, pardner."

I was also now working at the Dougherty's ranch, a fifty acre place across the road, owned by Bill, who had been the U.S. Russian ambassador in the 1940's, and his second wife Julie. I took over a few part-time jobs from Al Griego, the lifelong caretaker, who was married to Nellie, the housekeeper. Nellie made lunch for Bill every day. Al could no longer push the lawn mower around the manicured front grass and its sweeping grand entrance.

Probably the coolest thing I did for them was when Julie's son was getting married. He was professional mountain climber Carlos Buhler and by mountain climber, I mean Everest. So two hundred friends, family, and Sherpa's would be arriving for the reception. The mix of guests was eclectic, from local rowdies to elegant art patrons and the Dalai Lama. It was hard to say for sure, as he was wearing a Santa hat and sunglasses but we'd heard he was in town.

I hectically managed to valet park all the arriving chariots in a field behind the huge house, hidden, so every new attendee would think they were the first ones there. The guests were surprised when they went through the front archway to discover the grand ball Julie had created.

The party was complete with a strolling mariachi band strumming from fireplace-warm room to room. As I watched the last Range Rover of the night crawl out the farolito lined drive, I asked Julie if there was anything else she needed. She said, "Why, yes!" very matter of factly. "I invited ALL of them back for breakfast!"

Nellie was wearily picking up plates and shutting lights off as Al sat passed out in a big plush chair by the fire. She rolled her eyes like she did when Bill said that all he wanted for lunch was "tomato soup and a cracker." Seven o'clock the next morning they all showed back up to be greeted by the mariachi band. The Lama looked very hung over. Seriously.

Rockets on a Rope

Julie was a trip and my best time with her was bringing in a two story tall Christmas tree along with Al, Nellie, and Bill. We spent two hot chocolate toddy mornings decorating for another lavish annual holiday party. Yes, Julie certainly was a trip alright and I was about to get tripped.

Within two days after meeting Melissa was already pregnant and had moved into my bungalow. Julie came over one day and knowing of our predicament, predicted, "You can't have a baby in a trailer." I'd kinda figured it'd be alright until she was sixteen, or seventeen. "No!" she commanded. She ordered us to the guesthouse in the back of their place where she stored all of her family heirlooms. They were to be shuffled around and cleared out. We wouldn't pay rent. We'd just be available.

As I moved my stuff across the road I knew my life would never be the same again and it wasn't. One indication of how this worked out for them was the night around 3 a.m when the burglar alarm went off by accident. There were no burglaries in Tesuque because the burglars were too appalled by the wealth to even go there.

I crawled in through the locked door to the pantry by using the doggie door. Bill sat in the kitchen with his hands over his ears and gave me the thumbs up as I went to a back room to dismantle the blaring siren. "That's why you're here," he said, as I crawled back to the guesthouse. I'd wondered.

One day Bill asked if I wanted to drive him to the Land Association Acequia Madre Ditch committee meeting to be held in the tiny school gym. I had dutifully cleaned our portion of the five mile waterway, sculpted into the eastern hillside of most of Tesuque proper for many years and on many different properties. Built by the forefathers of the modern Tesuque clan, who now all lived in mobile homes out on the highway at the end of the ditch near the Casino. Oh right. They own the casino.

It was hard work traditionally handled by all of the men in the village together, one end to the other. Now due to legal restrictions, insurance liens, and huge gated walls around a lot of the places, it was kind of an "each man for himself" fiasco with many properties not even owning the water rights. Greedy real estate gophers had sold off in property transfers to golf courses - in a desert.

They were discussing annual dues as I stared out the window thinking about something else. Claudia most likely. I sort of heard it brought up that it was time for the election of the new Mayor Domo who made sure everything flowed smoothly. Shockingly, Pete Beasley had shot himself after moving back into my old place. So when the commissioner asked for volunteers or nominees, Bill chimed in, "Well how about Britt?" much to the dismay of Pat and Patrick and Bill's son, David. Few, if any, of the Spanish inhabitants who were present offered resistance. A small majority of hands sealed my fate.

Emily Grace was delivered by me and a midwife, standing by with a bottle of wine, on the early morning after Valentines Day on the futon in the guesthouse at the Dougherty Ranch in Tesuque, New Mexico to the Mayor Domo. Melissa dropped her out pretty quick and easily as I sipped the merlot.

Emily would spend every day from then on with me, crawling on the huge plastic tarps I pulled about the Hill's yard as a million cottonwood leaves came down in the fall.

I'd place her sleeping in an extra manure cart and I'd drag with me on my chores.

She would grow up in a pretty special neighborhood with an extremely diverse group of characters around her daily. She would learn to swim in the pool of the Duke and Duchess of Bedford, who had a vacation palace and a grand daughter Emily's age. She was about two.

Things had been alright up until then. Melissa was bored and frustrated with my constant recording of my own songs on some up-to-date digital equipment Terrence had bought me. The stuff was finally available to the consumer at this point for a mere fourteen thousand dollars. He said I didn't have to pay him back. A tip as it were.

The Hills were like Emily's Italian mob Godparents, showering her with expensive gifts from Rome and watching her in the house when I needed to do a dump run.

Bill and Julie were her real Godparents as well as Al and Nellie, her Spanish aunt and uncle. They all stood with us when we had her christened at the little church. Terrence and his wife Lori flew in from Rome and were the only real Catholics.

One day as Melissa, Nellie, and Julie were cleaning off the fine china, Julie decided, "We'll be having a wedding soon." My parents were actually driving out in a couple of weeks to visit their granddaughter and although Melissa and I both knew in our hearts we weren't right for each other, Julie assured us that it was in our daughter's best interest.

Now the ditch had been keeping me busy with twigs, log jams and new property owners who had no idea what was going on. Angry calls in the middle of the night, saying, "Where's my water? This is my time." Once at 3 in the morning a mysterious muffled voice said, "The market is flooding."

On that starlit, crystal clear night, I drove down to see water gushing down Griego Hill drive, an arroyo actually, and I drove up the raging current to the end of the road. A rusty steel culvert spanned over the arroyo carrying the sacred ditch. The source of the flood was coming from the south entrance to the huge pipe on Roger Miller's property.

I got out of the truck with a shovel, stepping into muddy flowing water, and climbed up the embankment, holding on to young cottonwood and elm trees to fight the current. When I got to the head gate, I saw a large 2 x12 piece of lumber had been hammered into the mouth of the span, an intentional blocking of the flow. Not sticks. or rocks, or mud. My heart raced as I suddenly heard Al Griego's advice to me when I was elected; "Don't get killed over a little bit of water."

Sliding back down the sloppy hillside after prying out the well-placed obstruction, I fully expected to hear a gunshot or run into some crazy hombré angry over something I didn't do.

The silence startled me as I got to my truck. The water was receding around me as I drove back down to the market that was still surrounded by a murky whirlpool filled with sticks, sand, rocks, and empty Bud Light cans and bottles.

The next morning Jerry, the owner of the market, gave me free breakfast, which was rare.

Very few people understood or cared about the job. Many Spanish families had maintained water rights for centuries but most of the newcomers were total city idiots. They had no idea how this beautiful valley had come about. It was like the water was just there by magic and the only reason their place was so expensive was because of the oversized, over-priced, crappy mansion. Not so. It was the water. It was really a burden.

We got married on a Saturday morning. Melissa wore a flower pattern dress, her hair in braids. I wore a white cowboy shirt and white corduroy jeans. Slim Green led Pandora in with my child's mother sitting sidesaddle. An intimate crowd of my parents, the "family" and assorted locals stood round as we were wed by a judge who would throw out drunk driving cases if you brought in a thanksgiving turkey for the homeless for bail.

We were given an important looking document to sign and present to the Magistrate Court within thirty days of the ceremony to make it official. We would never make it there.

One night I got a frantic phone call from a realtor who had just sold a new three million dollar place, built right smack on the ditch, to a woman named Ann. Upon just arriving in town today, she had opened the front door of her new flagstone home to find a cascade of water flowing through the empty building. In some places it was a foot deep. When I arrived I couldn't help but laugh at how much water had streamed through. "We're having a good spring. That's pretty impressive," I said as she stared at me in disbelief. The damage was minimal to the rock walls and rock floor. I stayed repairing the break in the ditch where the house had been built too close. And I forgot to call Melissa as I cleaned up the mud until about six in the morning.

The Ballad of the Mayor Domo

The next afternoon I told a bewildered Melissa I needed to check up on everything at Ann's place and make sure that the case was closed. It wasn't, as I ended up becoming involved with the woman who helplessly informed me she had millions and thought I should be working on my music and not tossing rocks in a ditch. And she was the secret child of an illegitimate political father figure. I fell for it...literally.

Melissa figured it out, I think, by the way I smelled. I came home one day to find all of my belongings had been moved back over to my trailer and my daughter and her mother were gone. Abruptly moving into the guesthouse at the Beasley's where the master of affairs, Val, had once resided, I got really drunk and went down to Andreas' pay phone to call Pat and leave an honest message as to how I felt about the situation.

I was met the next morning by two Police officers who handed me a year long restraining order and I was basically advised to "Get out of Dodge." Then I was met at the gates to Ann's place by two guys in suits and sunglasses who advised me to "Leave Ann alone!" Good suggestion.

I had traded a full year of free horse work at Debra's for an autographed John Lennon etching that was valued at $10,000. I knocked on the door of a billionaire neighbor who promptly gave me $6000 for it. Cash.

I stuck $3000 in the Beasley's mailbox and slid $3000 into Slim's wallet and, on the advice of my legal council, "Me, myself & I", decided to take a hike, literally. And I would never return to Tesuque like it was, because it would never be the way it was, again.

To Hell You Ride...

Now this feels like the end of the book for me, but it's not. It's really about horses, so we're gonna get to that soon, I promise, after one quick little trip.

I hitchhiked up to Telluride, Colorado where I'd always wanted to visit but not necessarily under these conditions. I would camp at a place I was told the real Butch and Sundance had plotted their famous first bank robbery. I burnt through my first $1500 real quick. It's not even worth explaining how or why, other than I didn't have anything else to do. Oh, I forgot to mention that Ann moved, disappeared, or vanished. I've never seen or spoken to her since.

After a couple weeks of contemplation, I figured I needed to get out of the gold mine town and decided I needed to head toward Colorado Springs if I wanted to find a new job or a new life. I encountered howling cold winds and spitting snows as the November elections grew near. It had the makings of a real fun adventure if it wasn't for the fact that I wasn't really having any fun. I was just missing Emily entirely, constantly, seriously.

Rockets on a Rope

As I crept into Creede one afternoon, a tiny mining town up in the crack of a canyon, I saw a young man sitting by a truck and horse trailer with his head in his hands and a pistol in a holster on the ground beside him. He said they called him "Jimi the Kid" and he'd been up packing with his two horses when something startled them causing a big commotion. The horse he was leading slipped and fell down a small ledge, breaking its leg. Jimi rode back to town to get his truck and his gun and asked if I wanted to "buy some beer" and tag along to help find the distressed horse. Since I had nothing impending I went along for the ride.

We drove high into the Colorado Rockies near the Continental Divide on a two-path rocky trail road until we came upon the still slowly breathing animal, his eyes open with a scared look. Jimi got out of the truck with the firearm and shakily walked over to his horse, started to cry, and stated, " I can't do it," handing the Colt 45 to me.

Since I had nothing else to do that afternoon, I placed the barrel against the forehead, just as Slim had explained, and sent the horse back to the barn. End of show.

As a reward for my bravery, Jimi drove me up to a sacred Ute hunting observation cliff and left me there drunk as a skunk, just enough to really not know where I was the next morning with about five hundred dollars left. This was getting to be an expensive vacation. Crawling into Colorado Springs, I got a newspaper and read how Clinton had got elected.

I saw a "Help Wanted" ad that read, "Over the road driver needed. Horse experience a must. Ready to travel immediately." So I walked to the business, All State Horse Express, with my backpack, some cigarettes, and what little money I had left from the now probably priceless Beatle's art work.

Rockets on a Rope

The truckline boss had a tight situation. His regular driver had a family crisis and wouldn't be able to leave the next morning for the seven day, seven thousand mile excursion around the western half of the continent. We would be picking up different horses and delivering them to and from numerous towns and stables.
"You know how to drive a big rig, right?" he quietly asked.

Seeing how there was no time for all the proper tests and licenses, etc., I said, "Sure."

He shook my hand and said, "You take off tomorrow. 6 a.m."

I asked if I could camp out by the semi in a stand of aspens. The deal was agreeable to both.

As I nervously ground the squealing first gear into second, sooner than I'd expected, early the next morning, my stage coach partner Walt, remarked, "You've never driven anything this big in your life, have you?"

Shift, shift, shift!

I told him how I pretty much hadn't driven anything for quite a while except for "Old Blue" and then looked at him like Steve McQueen in *The Getaway* and said, "I'll have it figured out by El Paso."

And El Paso it was, then Phoenix, San Diego, Santa Barbara, Los Angeles, Las Vegas, Salt Lake City, Bend, Seattle, Sun Valley, Cheyenne, Fort Collins, Denver, and back to home base, bringing one tired pony all the way around with us from El Paso.

To Hell You Ride...

It wasn't really playing with the horses as much as just driving nonstop. Seven hours on. Seven hours off. Trying to sleep in the back of the cab. Walt would wake up, automatically preaching, "Down shift! Down shift!" when he'd smell the brakes burning on a steep downhill, then fall back asleep, sort of. Oh sure there were heartwarming moments like the time there was a mother and daughter standing in the middle of the night, in the middle of the road, in the middle of somewhere with a horse, a suitcase and a bag of carrots.

Then somewhere in Wyoming, when the owner said, "She's kinda tough to load." After signing the travel orders and being asked to "Say goodbye", Walt and I locked arms to elbows, pulling a lead rope strung through a loop in the roof of the trailer, threw her in, and we were gone in a flash.

At one point we had thirteen horses in a twelve-horse trailer with the smallest one stowed in the trailer tack room. We never got them out and walked them around as was advertised. One especially painful part of the drive was going through L..A. on the back side of Beverly Hills, where I used to live, in a 7 mph traffic jam in 100 degree heat, the horses rocking the trailer from side to side. I climbed into the trailer with the travelers and used up all the carrots trying to keep them entertained. I also wiped everybody off with some cool towels I dipped in our ice chest as we slowly passed by the Burbank stables and now distant musical memories.

By the time we got back to Colorado Springs I'd had enough of the driving deal but I was told there would be another truck leaving for the east coast in a few days. I'd done a good job and was welcome to camp out until then and take the required drug and driving tests I needed by law to do what I had just done. I declined.

Rockets on a Rope

I decided I'd gotten enough money from that little excursion to head back to Telluride and give it another whirl. The cast of characters I encountered with a hand held out included two fourteen year-old twin brothers whose parents had gone out of town for the weekend. So they stole the truck, trailer, two horses and a bottle of Jack Daniels and went elk hunting. I jumped off in Pagosa Springs.

Next was a Christian couple who raised wolves. They took me over Wolf Creek Pass to their place in South Fork where I stayed for two days and helped stock fish ponds.

Then on to Salida with a phone repair man who'd seen me all over on his route and, although his company policy didn't allow him to pick up passengers, it was dark and he could tell I was late to someplace.

Then into Ouray with a seventy year-old woman whose conservative appearance was shattered when she offered me a joint from a cigarette pack that looked remarkably like J. Parti's. She had cataracts and said her relationship with her children had changed dramatically.

Last, but not least, was Jackson Browne driving to a benefit gig in Telluride. In a pickup truck with two girls, he brought me back into the wild west town that had swallowed my last bag of loot. I made three hundred bucks setting up chairs and moving guitars around for the show. I then proceeded to spend what I had like a five-cent cowboy in a ten-cent whore house, on Nickel Night.

When I was down to my last twenty bucks, I went into a fancy restaurant and ordered a fifteen dollar meal. When the extremely busy waiter brought the check back with five bucks change, I said, "I gave you a Fifty." He said, "Oh right."

To Hell You Ride...

As I walked out of the place with my last thirty-five, I couldn't tell if I was impressed or ashamed of myself.

Needless to say, I blew through that fast and, finally broke, was ready to surrender to the authorities. I called my parents collect from a pay phone on the highway just out of town and told them I was going hitch a ride home. I stuck out my thumb and the first guy who stopped had just "gotten out of prison" for something and hadn't really driven in 10 years.

"Where you heading?" I asked.

He offered, "Omaha." - One hundred miles away from the bedroom I grew up in.

That was an interesting trip.

Dad's last trip to Philmont

Rockets on a Rope

Returning to my childhood home was heartbreaking. I had my own child now and from the moment she was born I had been with her 24/7 for two years. We'd never ever even had gotten a babysitter. She went with me to work wherever I went and now I wasn't really even sure where she was or with whom.

Finding my kind of horse work in Iowa seemed hopeless with no movie stars or rich white women for at least a thousand miles in either direction. I missed New Mexico too. I had fallen in love with the beauty and unique way of life of the land and its people.

With nothing else to lose, I drove my dad's old van out to the Prairie Meadows racetrack, east of Des Moines. Standing in the grandstand before the upcoming race, I noticed a man in a black cowboy hat walking tersely out of the paddock area as the horses and jockeys entered the track for the warm-up jogs.

Rockets on a Rope

He came right up to some men standing behind me and loudly announced, "My damn Mexican showed up drunk again this afternoon. I had to bring this 'nut case' up myself." He gestured to the big gray thoroughbred trotting alongside an escort pony-rider. "I got two more races tonight and no help!"

I turned and mentioned to him, "I can work with horses."

"Well, can you now?" He asked.

I said, "Sure" and turned back to watch the action.
"No, I meant can you, NOW?!!"

He was on his cell phone speedily calling the Iowa Racing Commission office located under the grandstand, demanding, "I got a long-haired boy coming down right now." He shoved his arm in the air towards the tunnel way down. "Give him a temporary track pass, pronto!!" I heard him order as I took off running down a dark passage to the track office.

I was met by a fat woman who passed me a paper to read and sign. Something about drugs, liquor, licenses, and immigration status. Sure, I was from here. I signed it quickly. She handed me a badge. I felt like Wyatt Earp - Costner's version.

"What's up?" I declared as I ran back up to Marvelous Marv Johnson with my plastic clip-on backstage pass to the show.

He said "Go get your horse," pointing towards the losing gray soldier returning from the battle. "Walk him back about a mile, that way."

He pointed out into the humid evening air to Barn B.

Rockets on a Rope

"Kristen will meet you there and give you instructions." I ran down to the track pretty glad I'd had a few beers back in the casino. I arrived, flashing my badge to some fat guy, sitting at the track gate entrance.

I walked up to this huge, wet, bursting, throbbing, vein popping, racehorse, as the jockey slid off and cried, "Get the tongue-tie" pointing towards the missile's foaming mouth. There was a trickle of blood from the nose and I could see what looked like a shoe string cinched around the lower jaw, holding the tongue down. It was so they wouldn't inhale it as they came around the last stretch, I would be told later. As I released it, the horse jerked his head back and shook like he just woke up - after not waking up at the starting gate. The jockey (a trained monkey) ran off, no introduction. I steadied my hand on the reins and leaned my shoulder into the gray's. I took off with the heaving, soaking wet monster at a sideways jog. It was the longest mile I'd ever ran in my life, away from the lights and the bustle of the night time racing scene, down an ammonia smelling, wood chip road to the upcoming barn row ahead of us.

The barn was divided by rows of big mechanical hot-walkers standing like umbrellas without the fabric, empty now, except the apparent figure of a man hanging from his belt buckle, passed out where the horse was supposed to be, spinning slowly in circles like a drunken merry-go-round, piñata cowboy.

I continued into the first row of stalls down a long narrow hall. I saw Marv's wife waving at me saying, "Keep him moving. Keep going. All the way around the inside aisles" which were almost as big as a football field. Don't let him stop. Don't let him eat. Don't let him drink. And in about a half hour, start letting him have sips from a bucket hanging on this outside stall. "Cool him down slowly. You got all night. Right?" She ran off to lead another horse to the slaughter.

They raced in Iowa at night, probably because of the heat and humidity of the July corn roast. Racing ended at 10 p.m. The horses still woke up at 5 a.m., if they slept at all. We had been walking around an hour or so when Marv came back with the other horse. He asked if I was "doin' alright?" He told me to put mine away and gave me the other sweaty beast. "Do the same with him. I gotta run to the office before they close and clear things away on you." He returned just after midnight. "That's good. Put her away." We got out the long hose and watered everybody and Marv relinquished, "Let's get out of here."

"Hey did you get Pedro off suspension?"

We went out to find the struggling man awake, sort of, now bouncing up and down, as well as around. Marv unbuckled the chain and Pedro fell to the dirt. "Both of you be back here tomorrow at 5 a.m. Adios!" I introduced myself. Pedro asked if he could "borrow a cigarette." I gave him two and ran off.

"Morning, sunshine," I greeted everyone as I walked into the aisle of noise. Clanging stall doors, banging buckets, screaming inmates. Bales of hay had been stationed at each stall door by the hay fairy, apparently during the short night. Marv yelled, "Four flakes each. Just throw it at them." In a few minutes Pedro arrived, sort of, and went to pull out the grain cart, tossing in a couple coffee cans of grain each, more than I was ever told to feed anyplace else. Marv instructed me to repeat the watering process. "Then we'll get started." He bellowed: "Good morning, sunshine", I think to Pedro.

Rockets on a Rope

The crunching sound of the five square-mile facility filled the air. The energy level grew quickly as trucks began arriving and horses started spinning outside. "This side is yours. These are your horses," Marv pointed out, assigning me fifteen stalls. "After they eat, take your first four out to the walkers, then commence to mucking and don't dilly-daddle. Just strip them." I knew how to do that. The indoor racers had trampled whatever was in there to smithereens. Down to the rubber mat in a oatmeal blend of hay, urine, manure and wood chips (not expensive shavings) that I recognized from the walk back, the night before. Frantic two and three year-olds were spinning like zoo tigers in the 12 x 12 enclosure. They called them "indoor racers" and believe me, it made the chore exciting! Not having to properly pick, I cleaned them quickly as a familiar sweat returned. Putting on the first halter was a Max-like challenge.

These were squirrelly bastards and by that I mean, imagine a 1200 lb squirrel and put a halter on it! Marv showed me how to hook the young horses to the chain Pedro had been hanging from the night before. "Step back quickly and flip the switch" at the base of the diabolical device.

With a frightful lurch the horse squirmed on the chain like a hooked trout. "Go get your next horse now before this one gets lonely. And try to put your next one on the fly, so you don't need to turn the thing off." God forbid. That was a drag, but I got the hang of it. Soon a hundred or more trainees were flying in the morning dust, some kicking, some resisting, others wearily resigned to the simple circle.

I was shown the riding tack, a modest halter/bridle that looked like it offered little control and a girth with some stirrups, like Ralph's, only with a bicycle seat attached. There was a small leather pad called a "chamois" that

I was to carry with me when I took a horse up to the track. Marv and another warm-up rider took the individuals out as I went down the line doing chores and tacking up.

There was no racing tonight, otherwise the ones that were running that day would not have been fed. This was a good day to learn. I'd already figured out cleaning and feeding were not the art form they had been at Brightonwood. More of a shovel in/shovel out process.

My main job was to handle and prepare the horses in a manner that would "get them to the track alive" in Marv's words. He was a kind of a "If they win it's because of him. If they lose it's because of you" kind-a-guy. "And don't make pets out of my racehorses," he warned. "The mean ones win." And there were no carrots.

The next day there were dos X's on my stall doors, "Casino Nick" and" T.C. Diamond", a little gray mare that looked like a mule. Racehorse names could be deceiving and I made up a few of my own. "Don't" worked well because it was short and to the point and you didn't have to add "Remington" or "asshole" to the equation. "Trouble" was self-explanatory. These two would suffice and I tried to keep the discussions down to a minimum. The less they knew about your personal life around here, the better.

Now as it turned out, this was going to be Nicks last run, Marv's Hail Mary pass, as he had been struggling with stretched tendons in his front legs from trying too hard for most of the season. He was an expensive investment that "hadn't paid out", so Marv was squeezing one last attempt out of him. We applied a medical clay poultice to each leg, wrapped in saran plastic wrap. After a few hours I would spray them off and walk him a bit, before preparing for the duel.

I brought him back to the stall and started combing out his mane and tail and rubbing his body down with fly spray. Pedro came into my stall with a beer and a roll of black duct-tape. He told me, "Get the bridle on and be ready to go. Now just stand there" as he proceeded to tightly wrap the front legs with the industrial sticky tape from below the knee down. No pads, no cloth, no polos, no socks. Then he used red electrical tape to put two racing stripes near the top. That made them look pretty "Sporty"

I heard Marv order, "Get going now!" As Pedro slid the door open, we goose- stepped out. Nick was shaking his legs like a dog with a burr between his toes and then, within a few yards, he straightened out and we headed for the lights of the big time. Marv stared at the gelding's front legs as I paraded the horse around in front of the saddling area in the paddock. We did a few laps in front of the group of children, gamblers, onlookers and Mexican charros, who were standing by while deciding their best bets. "Pedro does a nice job," Marv surprised me, as the jockey showed up. I handed Marv the wet chamois as he strategically placed the small saddle.

"What do you need me to do?" Sanchez, the jockey, inquired.

"Uhhh. Run like hell and try to turn left," Marv suggested.

Sounded like a plan. As they rode off I moved over to the grooms gate, by the fat guy who nodded like he knew something I didn't.

At the finish line, where I would wait for the end of the race, Marv came up behind me and whispered, "If he wins, well, do what you're supposed to do...And if he doesn't, yeah, well, there will be a truck waiting back behind the barn.

Cool him off a bit and load him up..Oh, and give him a drink."
I could use a drink.

And they were off... Nick came out in a pack and I never saw him the whole way around. It was impossible and boring, even with the big screen TV at the bar. I never was that excited about the races anyway. I guess if it's actually your horse in the race it might be more interesting. Oh well.

As they came around the last turn, Nick was far in the back. Marv put his hand on my back as I went in to get him, saying, "Do as you're told, boy and go get T.C. up here." As we walked back to the barn and the waiting trailer, I could see most of the duct tape had ripped through, except the sporty red racing stripes, still holding on.

Did I mention T.C. Diamond looked like a damn mule and all of the other ponies used to laugh and call her names? I liked her because she was small and easy to push around in the shower stall. Marv didn't care too much about her. It seems his wife had traded a truck or something for her. Anyway, after I threw Nick away I didn't care. I was tired. I didn't want to be in Iowa and it wasn't my horse or decision. And I was missing Emily.

I got T.C. and took her up for a romp. I had my first "Winners Circle" photo taken with a new black hat that said "Marv Johnson Racing" on it. He handed it to me as I led her in after we had won. The little horse that looked like a mule and I had passed the audition. I could make Marv money and the hat proved it. The next morning there was a box of donuts.

There were also two new X's on my stall doors. M&M and Magin' Matt. Now the prize from the night before was actually $10,000 and it turns out Marv's wife had secretly bet $5000 on her own, which added up to $60,000 for winning the one race with the odds she had. So I learned real quick that betting a dollar got you nowhere. But if you went for it you could buy a foreclosed house. I wasn't into betting. It hadn't worked out that well in Telluride and I could tell there were way more factors involved than just who had the fastest ride: The whole circumstance of the situation, the noise, the hours, the little jockeys playing backroom games. The same jockeys rode all the races, every evening. They just switched around, working for all the different trainers at will. Now this "Sanchez" who had rode Nick to hell and did workouts for us had exercised my lovely M&M, a petite chestnut filly. He knew she was timid, head shy and seemed the "least likely to win a race" horse, which is why I loved her the most.

Sanchez wouldn't be riding this race for us. He'd be on "River Ridge Rowdy" this go round and it was to be a tough pack. M&M's odds were wild and I decided to put the thousand dollars I had managed to save down on her. Marv had told me she was fast enough as long as she got out of the gate ok. She was very head shy and didn't like mud on her face., so if she got behind, she stayed behind - way behind. If not, I'd make enough money to go back to Tesuque and buy my own shack. As I went in to prepare her, she nuzzled me like she didn't understand why I hadn't fed her that morning. She paced around the stall as I tried to shine her up.

When they came out of the gate I actually saw Sanchez on a big gray beside M&M swing the whip in his hand far out to the right in front of my horse's eyes. She pulled up, then stumbled and stammered back behind the herd. As the group came around the last turn, I could see her loping along on the outside rail as if in a pasture on a spring day. Marv actually claimed later she was looking at and drifting toward me, ready to go home, as she crossed the finish line.

I went to get her and unleash her tongue. Sanchez, who had just won, rode by. "You touch one of my horses like that again and I'll break your little wetback neck!" I yelled. He rode off laughing. Marv said, "You're a groom. You're not supposed to talk to the riders like that. But he don't speak that good of English so he probably figures you just said 'nice ride'." On the long walk back to the showers she nuzzled me like we were in a Lassie movie, acting like "Timmy, what happened? Did we just lose the farm?" I cooled her down, gave her a couple carrots I'd smuggled in and tucked her in for the night. I did hope she ended up as some rich little white girl's show jumper.

I went to get Maggin' Matt, Marv's pride and joy, a big bay with a bold white and brown blaze. I'd been told to wear all blue that night and my company hat too. Marv and his wife and kids were also wearing blue and unbelievably Sanchez was riding. Apparently we were going to win and I obviously had chosen the wrong horse to bet on.

I looked in my empty wallet from Slim. I walked to the stall. He was beautiful. Slim, I mean, and the horse too - a warship, hard to handle and as solid as any horse I'd ever seen. I'd gotten along fine with him. He was a lot like Max, too big and too smart for his own good. I brushed him up, stimulatingly fast. He looked great just standing there. We bridled up and headed up to the Coliseum.

Night races were crazy. You could feel the horse tense up as you walked into the lights and the Lost Vegas atmosphere. As we were saddling, an announcer with a microphone talked to the crowd. He walked up to Marv asking, "What makes you think you've got a chance?" Marv shrugged his shoulders on the big screen TV and said, "Well I don't know! It's a horse race-race-race" which echoed throughout the whole place-place-place.

Sanchez strode out three feet shorter than me, with his little whip under his armpit, and suggested, "I won't even have to slap him for you, Marvy" as he looked at me, smiling. Well, surprise, surprise, surprise... We won, easily, and it was a fast race. Marv slapped me on my back as my hat flew off and said, "There you go, horse whisperer. See what your training has done. That's your horse, man. We won. Go get him...And tell Sanchez, 'Thank you'."

I saw all of Marv's kids scurrying to the winners circle like blue Nebraska bunnies. It's like he'd planned a Christmas card photo. When the camera clicked, Matt stood up straight on his hind legs and Sanchez slid off his butt into Marv's arms. We trotted off into the darkness and to the vet barn for dope testing.

When you win you have to go there. Also to the Lasix barn, which is where they administer and check for the drug that helps to keep their lungs from bleeding. (?) Now Matt had peed on the way up, something you get them to do by whistling on the way. And it works, sometimes. So we ended up walking around whistling for another two hours while a vet tech followed us around with a silver bucket. They actually turned the lights down and played soft music to try and relax him after the other winners had left. It was after midnight when finally he stopped, stood back, and dribbled out a specimen. And there were photos and donuts for everybody in the morning.

Rockets on a Rope

My dad would be bringing my Uncle Chuck, who was now in his eighties, to the track that next night.. He was pretty blown away by the number of horses in all the busy barns and was rather surprised I was working with horses at all. So was I.

A new horse came that day in a trailer from California. Some big deal Marv had traded for babies. His name was "Unlimited (something)". There had been some viruses running around the west coast tracks that summer, so Marv told me to take him to the showers with a gallon jug of Clorox (My mom would be proud) and hose him down.

Straight off the trailer, this horse was NUTS. A huge dapple gray with a salt and pepper mane. Psychotic. Even with a chain over the upper gum, under his upper lip. He pushed into you, over you, and liked to bounce more than trot. ..sideways. He appeared to be on the edge most of the time. After a few days of training, Marv concluded that he wore himself out on the trip up to the gates.

In short races he tended to come back on strong at the end, meaning he'd actually probably do better in longer races. I'm not quite sure how that works. If he wasn't blowing off so much energy to begin with, he'd win. Sounded like a plan. (Almost "Kilmer-istic".)

As I was trying to clean him up for the evening outing, Marv came by and said, "In exactly five minutes (looking at his watch) put his bridle on, then turn your back to the door and when you hear it open, don't turn around. When you hear it close, count to ten. Then head on up. I'll be waiting for you."

That was pretty suspenseful. I did as I was told and, sure enough, in exactly five minutes the door slid open. I heard a pat on the neck. The horse jerked back as the door slid shut. I counted to ten. Then the horse relaxed and stood still. "Get going...Now!" Marv screamed.

I opened the door and he came out like a kid's pony. He trotted along with me nicely, snorting and drooling a bit. The mile hike to the track was uneventful but as we entered the parade paddock he shook his head, breathed a heavy sigh, and woke up. We lurched into the arena. The crowd cheered as he pranced sideways like a madman. Uncle Chuck was impressed and went off with my dad to bet money on him.

He stood pretty good as Marv tossed the saddle and jockey on. "What was that you gave him?" I asked. Marv looked straight at me and said, "I didn't give him anything and you didn't see anything." He was right, as always. He didn't win that night but did a lot better. I was glad I didn't have to go to the drug barn. I was sorry about my uncle's money.

The next morning the track preacher, who gave a little prayer every morning and rambled on and on the barn PA speakers about being careful, came on sounding quite different. He solemnly announced that "one of us hadn't been listening to him" and a groom had been killed the day before. That was sobering, sort of. Not surprising...or uncommon, or publicized.

There actually was a drug bust that week too. A big sheriff's bus came in and loaded up a bunch of grooms from an enemy barn. One of their horses had tested positive for cocaine of all things. Apparently the sweat exchanged in the contact between horse and groom, shoulder to shoulder like Siamese twins, could transfer.

Rockets on a Rope

Speaking of transfer. As the racing season in Iowa wound down, Marv asked if I wanted to stay on and go to Arkansas, the next step to the Kentucky Derby. That wasn't really the direction I was going and I only had two more months on Melissa's restraining order.

So I took a fill-in position with a thoroughbred breeder horse I had met at the track called White Dove. It was the home of a retired champion named Commemorate, a likable enough fellow I was told had been involved in some of the famous Alydar/Affirmed grudge matches. His family tree came down from Northern Dancer/Native Dancer, a very popular breeding stock line in the midwest. He was easy going, went with the program and was not much to write home about at his age.

The other stallion, Quaker Hill, was another story. A fire-breather and habitual biter and an aggressive fighter, he'd won the Canadian Derby, then blew his legs out. He was descended from Alydar who, rumor had it, had killed a Mexican groom (undocumented). And I had to sign a release saying I understood his nasty nature.

It took two grooms to even get his halter on safely. One would enter with a chain held between both hands as the stallion attacked, biting down on the chain. Then the other guy would put the halter up over that and attempt to get him harnessed. Then with two people with lead ropes on either side, we'd escort him out to his extra high-fenced exercise pen. It wore you out just getting him out.

My dealings with him were kept to a minimum but I mention him, for he was the basis for the term "Rockets on a Rope", which I thought pretty well described his situation. I guess what I took from my experience from him was this:

Rockets on a Rope

Unlike a gelding or a mare, a stallion was fully aware that he was way bigger than you and used that to his advantage and was basically a dominant animal that easily could seriously hurt you or kill you just playing around. I've heard of breeding barns where super-aggressive stallions are moved from place to place through a series of sliding door panels., almost like the Panama Canal, where the horse is never actually handled by a person.

What I did enjoy the most at White Dove was playing with the babies stalled directly across from their mothers, each with their father's looks and personality easily observed. Every day, after the usual feeding and cleaning, I would groom each one, carefully picking up each foot to clean out the bottom of the hoof to get them familiar with the routine. Working horses have their feet cleaned often. And baths too. Because of all the salt they sweat out running that hard. they had to have baths, like it or not, or their coats would almost crystalize. Then clean their eyes, their ears and wipe their nose. Brushing out the bushy mane and tail, I was just generally getting them used to being handled.

In the afternoons, they would be led one by one to the large Iowa pastures where they raced together like flock of starlings. It was inspiring and breathtaking but also a sad indication of where their young lives would lead. My year-long stay in Iowa had finally elapsed. I headed back to New Mexico in my Dad's old '75 Chevy van.

The Map to Tucson

Happily I returned to Santa Fe for a momentary visit with my daughter in the church parking lot in Tesuque. I soon discovered all my past jobs had been taken by Melissa's new boyfriend, John. Quite a few of the Tesuque residents had died or moved off to Montana. Or the next beautiful hip place to be destroyed.

I was told by a friend to check out the new Santa Fe horse park as there was a training barn looking for a traveling groom. I was greeted by Caroline, the stable manager, and mother of the hunter/jumper instructor, Sarah. Flying under the banner... Invicta.

I was told they'd be leaving for Tucson, Arizona the next morning at 5 a.m. After explaining my experience to date, I was hired again on the spot. I always wondered who had been doing the job the day before.

I camped out in the parking lot that night and woke up the next morning to the sound of two trucks with trailers arriving at 5 a.m. Sarah would end up reminding me a lot of the racehorse Unlimited. She wasted a lot of time and energy in preparation for something, came on strong at the end, but never finished where she really wanted to be.

She hardly noticed me as she stalked into the barn flipping on the lights to be greeted by the early morning requests for breakfast.. The other driver, Clayton, was her cowboy boyfriend. He introduced himself and suggested, "So you're the new slave, huh?" He gestured for me to follow and we began loading five horses per trailer.

A group of sleepy-eyed young ladies arrived next and trickled into the barn, completely unaware that I was there. All the hay, tack, and supplies had been put in the day before. So when the last horse was loaded, Sarah said, "You guys get going and set everything up when you arrive. We'll follow a bit later in the Land Rover."

Clayton asked, "How do we find the stalls?" Apparently disgusted, Sarah immediately crouched down and began drawing a detailed map in the parking lot dirt, taking us from Santa Fe (including gas stations and rest stops) all the way to the entrance of the Tucson fairgrounds.

She looked up at Clayton, who dryly responded, "Ok, you got us to the fairgrounds. Now how do we find the stalls?" It was like he'd asked her what time it was and she described how a watch works.

Right then Caroline drove up with some paperwork: Coggins tests, vaccines etc. They described each horse's color and distinctive marking and were to be presented at the state line Livestock Inspection Station. She said, "I couldn't find everything exactly but these should work." As Clayton got last minute instructions, I flipped through the documents listing a few paints, an Appaloosa, some ponies, and nothing that really described the ten, mostly brown travelers we were transporting. Whatever!

The Map to Tuscon

Now the best part of the trip was stopping to fill up with gas and dropping the trailer windows down to let the horses have a breath of fresh air and a sip from a bucket. Excited shouts came from traveling children who had apparently never seen a horse. They'd laugh as the horses knocked the bucket I was holding up, spilling most of the water on me.

I sat nervously at the border inspection station while a fat guy in a sagging uniform with a badge hardly looked at the trailer, barely looked at the papers, and never saw the horses. Homeland Security (pre-2001). Sarah had asked us to get the horses out halfway for a walk, just like the All-State Express.

To which Clayton responded (to me), "Are you kidding?" We proceeded into Arizona and, upon arriving at our destination, unloaded. Then we began putting up the banners, stall curtains and feed cards. Six bags of compressed shavings had been placed in front of each stall and I emptied them in as Clayton placed the horses according to importance, apparently because Sarah's horse, Santa Fe Silver ("Scotty"), was first.

When the troop arrived, the girls began unloading saddles and trunks of expensive riding apparel. The place began to take on the feeling of the racetrack crossed with a girl scout camp.

We placed the hay in a designated feed stall that would double as my sleeping quarters the next week. The first day I was kept busy setting up and acquainting myself with each ride, learning the individual saddles, with breast collars to keep the expensive seat from falling off. The bridles had a bit more message than M&M got at the track.
I walked Scotty around to scout out the place. Multiple

arenas, bathing areas, on-site vets, farriers and medics. Warm-up and cool-down paths. Burrito busses and acres of high-dollar RV's and Cinzano umbrellas, much like the track walkers, only with fancy fabric. And Margaritas.

Now another interesting observation to me, not Scotty, was the fact that none of the white people spoke to me in as much as even nodding to me or apparently noticing me. I would assume my long hair in a pony tail, beat-up cowboy hat, and cigarette in my mouth threw them off. The Mexicans never raised their eyes to me either. Obviously just because I was a white groom.

Today was set-up, tomorrow warm-up, Thursday preliminary, Friday and Saturday "The Show", and Sunday pack up and go home. The first night's feeding was new. Bute for everyone. A few got Banamine cocktails given intravenously in the neck, which was a first for me but I'd seen it done.

That evening, after the kids had gone back to the Hilton, Clayton dropped by, on his way out of town with a 12-pack of Bud Light, to submit his letter of resignation. He was going back home to attend to the main barn and he wished me "good luck" which I certainly accepted. Then he responded, "No, I really mean good luck."

After a relatively good night's sleep on some shavings, bags arranged neatly in the corner of my stall, I awoke around 5 a.m. to what sounded like a Mariachi band playing pretty closely in the distance, echoing through the fairgrounds, mixed with the early cries of equine beggars. As my group began to shuffle, I got going with a Mountain Dew in one hand and a cigarette and water hose in the other. I started refilling the buckets that had been drained after the long drive into "Tombstone".

The Map to Tuscon

Scotty began to pound on his door. He was Sarah's "A" ticket ride and she had informed me that she was one of the best riders in the world. In the meantime she was giving lessons and getting paid to yell at little kids, whose fathers were completely paying for these little excursions into the desert Southwest.

The Land Rover pulled up just as I wrapped up mucking and sweeping the barn aisle - the Red Carpet treatment. I heard the youngest girl Katie run from the truck to greet her prize pony, Lady, who was showered with pats, hugs, kisses, and carrots. Her older sister Amanda stepped out of the truck like the Queen of England.

She walked straight past me and her big black horse Paladin, straight into the tack/dressing room. Katie brushed, stroked and saddled her own horse. "Damanda" emerged from behind the curtain in shiny knee-high boots and top-of-the-line riding attire and secured her maroon velvet helmet. She requested,"Is my horse ready?"

"Ready for what?" I asked. "He's eating." I heard Katie giggle in her stall. Sarah arrived promptly and said, "Don't worry about mucking."

She continued, "You can do that tonight on your time off!" ...?

"Put Paladin in the cross ties and get them going."

By this time Katie was already trotting around the warm-up ring in front of the barn. Sarah walked out to her, screaming, "You're ruining that horse! Don't lead her like that! Let her have her head. She knows more than you." Perhaps she was talking to herself.

Katie was eleven and actually five years younger than the horse, who was a proven show veteran known by many of the "enemy" troops. Red-faced Katie breathed hard as she repositioned herself in the saddle and aimed for the three-foot jumps scattered in some pattern inside the giant arena. "She's a guaranteed winner," Sarah fired back up. "You're gonna screw her up if you keep telling her what to do, I'm gonna take that horse away from you." Katie stared at Sarah like Rocky.

It turns out their father had purchased both former champions. Each had won countless shows for countless other little girls and ending up with these two - both adopted and as different as night and day.

As Damanda approached, I tightened Paladin's girth and pulled down the stirrups. She handed me her Jackie Onassis glasses and took the reins. "Leg up," she expressed, staring at me and lifting her right leg at the knee, as she held the saddle.

"Put your hands together like this," she sighed as she bowed over. I mimicked her move as she stepped into my hands and said, "Lift." I tossed her up onto the large horse. Without a "thank you" they leapt out of the barn. I looked at the dirt on my guitar playing hands. This was interesting.

Katie swept into the barn aisle breathing excitedly. "She's awesome!" She squealed, "I love her to death." The two looked inseparable as she slid down and kissed Lady's muzzle.

After removing her own tack and leg pads, she politely asked, "Can you run her down to the bath while I change into my muckers?"

"Delighted, madam," I bowed.

The Map to Tuscon

Gladly I scampered the pampered pony to the showers where a group of Mexicans were spraying their horses and each other in the hot desert sun. None spoke to me and the horseplay ceased when I washed my pony off. When we returned, Katie had mucked the stall again, replenishing it with an extra bed of shavings? And a bucket of carrots.

Damanda blasted in on a hot, foamy Pal and threw the reins at me as she stormed off to a press conference or something. I removed his tack and proceeded to the hoses again. This time, as I arrived with Paladin, the other guys noticed - the horse. They watched as I sprayed him down. With a cigarette in my mouth, I smiled and nodded. A few nodded back.

After the Banamine party, I strolled out of the barn area and found a convenience store and got some smokes, some beer and some Dole bananas. I returned to my stall and drank the beer alone, missing my own little girl to the sound of banging buckets and farting horses.

The next morning I awoke to the same music, which always seemed to disappear by 7 a.m. I was beginning to get used to it, even cha-cha-ing goofily as I filled the water buckets.

After breakfast I was preparing all the horses as the troops walked the course while Sarah explained what they were going to do wrong. One by one the girls came back to get their mounts, each one with a different variation on the "Leg up?" and a minimal thank you. Katie handed me a McMuffin she had stuck in her jacket. I got no response from her sister as I blurted out, "Morning, princess," both of us, I guess, half believing it.

Today was preliminary, with no eliminations. Scoring would dictate final classes for the show. I smoked while the kids were gone and picked at the stalls all day. Thanks, Ariana. Sarah had informed me I was not to leave the barn area. By early afternoon the girls began returning with their tired horses and a few red, white, and yellow ribbons. Katie was thrilled with Second Place and proudly hung her ribbon on Lady's stall door.

After dinner I drank my beer and decided to hang all the brightly colored trophies on each door to liven things up a bit. With all the colors flapping in the sandy breeze, I crawled off to sleep. The next day Sarah was first down the narrow walkway, methodically ripping down the consolation prizes, throwing them in the dirt and screaming,"Nothing but blue today. Do you hear me? Nothing but blues!" I swear.

Although I never left the horses or saw the girls compete, the next two days went smoothly for all. Katie and Lady had qualified for regional championships and we ended up with an even mix of First and Second Places that seemed to satisfy Sarah enough to continue her burden.

The trip back to Santa Fe was uneventful. I was told I'd done well and would be needed again for Flagstaff in two weeks. I was allowed to stay in the parking lot in my van. I spent the days grooming and saddling for daily lessons, getting to know the horses and riders and continued to get better with wrapping legs for bed, then grooming them to perfection in the morning.

Show Jumping

Flagstaff, it would turn out, was more of an endurance show to weed out the undeserving participants. It was hailing as we arrived at the rodeo grounds in a huge pine forest. The place was flooded with mud and littered with sagging portable tent stalls. Incredible all night lightning displays prevailed. No matter how great the horses looked in the tents, getting them to the indoor arena without a splashing of mud would be impossible. Sarah assured me "it wasn't a beauty pageant." I did the best I could and hoped she informed Damanda of the circumstances, however obvious. With the cold and damp came the additional chore of blankets on/blankets off. I quickly learned to make this one of Ariana's jobs that had to be completed, before getting on to my job. Each horse went out as shiny as possible and came back as muddy as you can imagine.

The first morning, because of the sloppy conditions, I led Paladin with Damanda on board, up to the warm-ups. As I bent over to remove the horse's polos, I was struck in the back of the head by a muddy boot. Startled, I looked up and I saw a jolly looking Mexican fellow nearby, who tossed me a semi-clean rag and made a shoeshine motion with a serious, stern, almost inner reflection kind of look. I caught on and tried to wipe away as much of the mess as possible from both boot and sole. As they rode off, Je'sus laughed at me and said, "You need to spit on her boot to get the whole experience, primo!"

That night, as I wrapped up feeding in a biblical rain storm, solemnly slipping back towards my tent. Je'sus beckoned me like a shining light.

"Ese' primo, amigo. Come with me, friend. They're making you a feast."

I followed him around to a steeple-like covering where all the other grooms had gathered, bent over like monks, wrapped in ponchos, spiritually slicing tomatoes and avocados and sacrificing chickens in huge pots of beans and rice. He offered me a Dos XX' s cerveza and said, "Come. Drink with us, pilgrim. You're a hard worker and you have all the best horses. Besides, you have taught us about prejudice," he preached. "We once believed that we were treated like crap because we were wetbacks. You have shown us it's because we are grooms... And forever shall be... Amen."

We ate, drank, and laughed as Je'sus began to "show" me the Spanish I needed to know and recite the professional groom's scout oath: "A horse is a horse of course, of course, unless he's worth a million dollars." I learned "Ese primo" was "Hey cousin", "Mira Vato" was "Look dude", and the always popular, "Mucho trabajo piquito dinero" - "Much work, little money".

As we each wandered back to our respective camps, we shouted, "Manana, manana. The sun'll come up, manana."

Show Jumping

I suddenly felt part of a minority brotherhood. I had become one of them. I was a "Professional Mexican."

Sarah informed me the next morning was the big day. I would be needed at the show ring early with Paladin and another horse, "Daddy's Money", that Amanda was basically test driving for when Pal gave in. Or gave out? Or gave up? I was needed for the switch.

As I watched her ride the first horse, I saw her neck snap as they came out of the corners and her shoulders slumped way too closely to the horse's head. She looked uncomfortable at best. What she lacked in riding skill, she made up for with an educated horse.

Je'sus was standing nearby with his patron and offered, "You need to put a better rider on him. That horse can win."

"Yeah, well. That wasn't part of my job description." I shook my head as I went to retrieve Paladin and gave Amanda Daddy's Money.

Sarah had begun to notice I had been born again. With shouts of "ese' primo" coming at me from all directions now. And I was returning the blessing. She told me there was a pizza party that night in the show ring and I could come if I cleaned up and didn't bring my nuevo amigos. I assumed it was some kind of white-tie affair and since I didn't have any clean clothes, I fired up the golf cart we had rented and decided to retrieve as many starving charros as I could round up. Je'sus cried out to the heavens, "Ieeee andele'yeyea", leaning as we rounded the corner leading into the Pavilion with a fiesta-like tune playing loudly on the radio. We pulled up to the tables like a pack of dogs. We grabbed quite a few pizzas really, before stealing off into the night air like Pancho Villas' raiders.

The last morning of the show I could tell Sarah was not amused. She disapproved of my smoking and drinking, but I got things done. I was doing a great job. The horses responded to me well and the kids liked me. We were winning consistently and the parents saw me as sort of a camp counselor, maitre'de, and janitor figure. All the girls had qualified for the final season championships to be held in Scottsdale in November, the week of Thanksgiving. So I returned to my parked van to groom and exercise my charges for the next three weeks and realized I was actually getting good at this horse thing.

"Underground Tuscon"

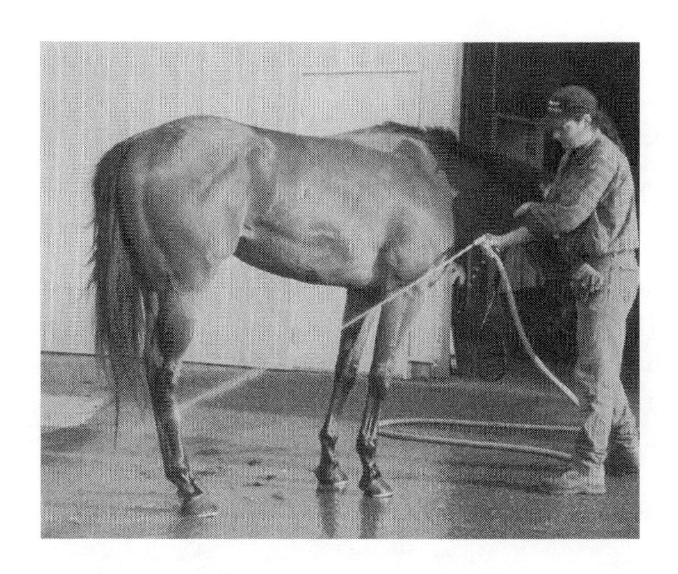

The Legend of the Great White Groom

A large horse transport passed us as we were nearing the Scottsdale exit on the highway. As the end of the trailer reached my driver's door, the last window on the rig popped open and a joyous Je'sus climbed halfway out waving and crying, "Ese' primo! See you at Scottsdale." I switched the radio station to K-Taco and anticipated the party.

I thought it was enlightening that he was in the back of the bus with the burros while there was only one gringo driving up front. Personally I was really starting to enjoy the abuse myself! Scottsdale was a mammoth affair with indoor and outdoor arenas and stadiums for miles. It seemed like it was it's own little city with cafes and bars. And the Police.

The first afternoon a calvary patrol mounted cub scout rode into my aisle and asked me, "Are these your horses?" I didn't know how to respond so I answered, "No Habla' englees." Je'sus had told me to confess if the Romans approached.

Rockets on a Rope

The officer stared at me, kinda stern, kinda serious, no inward anything, and said they were executing a riot training drill that evening.

"Down in the main parking lot, not that far away," he advised, "at oh, 1900 hours. Before you go back to your hotel, batten down the hatches. Stay with your best or spookiest horse and be ready to call the vet if something goes wrong." Thank you, Deputy Fife.

"This *is* the hotel. We'll be fine. Thanks for the warning."

I ran to the store and grabbed some beer. I ran back to the barn and made the brilliant decision to give them all a small shot of Banamine and a beer. No Bute, no doubt. Thank you Jesus! We got ready for armageddon. I was kneeling in front of Lady, next to Paladin. In the silence, as much as there can be silence, at a horse show.

I heard two or three low flying helicopters incoming over the stable. Lucky the wise man had told me of it. This seemed like it was going to be fulfilling. I could swear I could hear the theme song from the TV show *M*A*S*H*. Barely, suddenly, huge explosions rocked the arena. Loud screaming and fireworks followed. There were actually people dressed like hippies carrying protest signs and throwing aluminum cans filled with rocks, for Christ's sake. This was nuts.

A few of my horses snorted and spun in their stalls. One freaked out totally and one slept through it. My two stood bravely beside me as if they'd done a tour of duty here before. So all this went on for forty-five freakin' minutes, then...just stopped. They all shook hands and went home for Thanksgiving. Just another day at the office.

As the smoke cleared and the dust settled, nobody dropped by for a body count or to check on the wounded. I heard a few people talking and a couple of vets driving around as I lay on my sleeping bag with my boots on. I figured all might not have gone as planned, collateral damage and such. Still I went to sleep with a good conscience now knowing all my horses were, yes, a little edgier, but also more hip, if you see what I'm saying.

The next morning came quick and, although a few of my herd were a bit groggy and unsettled, all in all we were ready to rock & roll. After doing all my chores and before prepping the first horse, I went out front for a spliff and a Dew as a big Mercedes rolled up and Damanda stepped out. "Good morning, Britt. Are you working today?" she said in a tone that sounded a whole lot worse than it reads.

That was it. I'd finally had enough of her belligerence and I said to her sharply, "Look, you're not my daughter, my girlfriend, my mother, or my wife. You talk to me like that again and I'll grain your horse up so high you'll think you're at the Rodeo. And be nice to your little sister. She's a way better rider and just overall better person than you."

I spun around to walk away, only to see her father standing twenty feet back. I was thinking about where my next new job might be and tried to ignore him and look like I had someplace else to be. As I passed by he said, "Britt?" As I turned to face my fate, he stuck out his hand with a rolled up fifty dollar bill in his sweaty palm and said, "Thank you. I wish I could talk to her like that. You're doing great job, considering."

Katie came into my stall a couple minutes later and put down a pack of Camels, which I don't smoke, and said,

"Here. I found these in the parking lot". I said, "Thank you. You're the best." That evening Je'sus came by carrying two six-packs. Some new guys were having a fiesta in the next door aisle and we were invited to drop by.

There was a surprising amount of beer around there. More than I would expect, especially on the night before finals. We laughed, we talked, and I began to realize every time I was done with one beer, some hombre would inevitably hand me another. Andele,'Ala! It appeared as though they were trying to get me drunk... or drunker than normal.

Upon concluding this to be true, I excused myself, "Uno momento", saying I needed to go put water in a beet pulp solution to soak, which they thought was cool. So I went back to an empty stall and puked up everything in me, a trick I'd learned from an L..A. model I dated for 3 years, who drank white wine all day long and didn't eat. I then returned to the fire for more. Just like my daze with Val. I did this a few more times. Pretty soon there were Mexicans falling every which way, singing and dancing and passing out.

Je'sus figured out what I was doing and said he had heard one of the drunks mention that his patron or boss had actually purchased the beer and had instructed her grooms to get me drunk which, considering my years with Crosby, Stills & Nash, my high metabolism, and healthy diet of Mountain Dew and cigarettes, didn't really work out too well for them.

I told Je'sus, "Adios" and headed back to my barn at 2 a.m. and decided to just stay awake, go back to work, sober up, and have everything shipshape by 7:00. As I entered my aisle one of the drunk bastards was poking his fingers at

Paladin claiming, "I know this caballo. This was my horse. I know him. I say he was the Mexican National Grand Prix champion."

"Get away from him," I demanded. "Leave him alone. Go home!"

He said he was sure it was the same horse and started to open the stall door. I pulled out Roberts Redford's clippers and, sticking them into the flabby side of his belly, clamped down on his intoxicated flesh as he squealed and crumbled to the floor.

Je'sus heard the disruption and came running to see the squirming man with a blood spot on his sweaty t-shirt. "Que pasa? Did you shoot him? Eee-che-wowow!" I held up my trusty clippers to which his red eyes sprang open! He made a grimace, somewhere between a smile and repulsion.

"El Tigre," he saluted as he drug the man back to his aisle and I went back to my job. That worked out well. Half the fellows were still asleep and their horses hungrily crying when the troops arrived at dawn.

Jesus stopped by on the way to someplace the next day and said Pal really was the Mexican National Grand Prix champion like maybe fifteen years ago, but it didn't matter now and that unfortunate poker player was still asleep too.

Katie was the first to ride in the day's events. Because of the bond we had developed that summer, it was decided I would escort them to the ring, like a full-blown professional groom, horse, rider team. I was delighted as I led Lady down the road to the arena. Katie followed 10 paces behind like a boxer going to the ring. Like Elvis and his body guards.

I gave her a leg up, which she had never requested, and handed her a bottle of water as we waited. I walked around the horse a couple of times meticulously picking at her like a mother chimpanzee. I stroked her tail out with my hand and wiped Katie's boots off - no spit, no shit. I then cleaned Lady's feet out with a hoof pick I now had attached to my belt.

As she entered the warm-up ring for a couple of spins, Sarah added, "Give her her head." The two entered the arena and cleared the first two obstacles in a calm, accurate, steady flow. As they came around a turn, directly in front of us I saw Lady's ears flip back at the rider in a manner horses do when they're angry, distracted, or confused. Sarah growled, "Don't tell her what to do." At that moment Lady stopped dead in her tracks. Katie flew like a rag doll into the wooden jump and onto the dirt. I looked at Sarah, who motioned me to go get the horse who was standing right beside her fallen partner. The medics, Sarah, and Dad, all ran out to the shaken rider, now sitting up and covered in dirt. Dad pointed for me to take the horse out. Sarah snapped, "Get back up there. She's not hurt and they're not done yet."

Katie, kind of crying now, stood up dusting herself off as everyone inquired as to her condition. "She's fine," Sarah informed us. "You totally caused that yourself," she told the rider, now remounted. The medic walked up behind me and whispered, "I don't care what Cruella DeVille says over there. Is your rider good to go?"

"Katie?" I asked. "Are you all right?" Everyone paused.

"I could use a cigarette and a whiskey right about now," she said seriously.

As they jumped back into the game, no one said a thing, not even Sarah.

We won everything that day. No kidding. All the classes. All the stall doors were decorated in blue as we happily took down our flying colors and began to load up.

Before Je'sus drove away, he stopped his truck, ran out and handed me an empty beer bottle with a rose in it and a label that said in magic marker, "Best Of Show." I hugged Katie, and even Amanda, as I finally felt a true part of the horse world.

My jeans had been replaced by green cargo pants with a multitude of pockets. My old cowboy hat had been replaced by a smart regional championship cap, turned backwards, and my leather gloves had given way to high-tech spandex deerskin - useable ones. You could put on a bridle, undo a latch and light up a smoke without having to take them off.

Clayton called and said there was a problem with the second truck. I would have to remain that night with the second five horses, with just enough hay and a hose, and no money. Tomorrow was Thanksgiving Day.

I walked back to the barn, opening the empty stall doors to make sure nothing was left behind. I looked into Lady's stall under a show t-shirt. There was a 12-pack of beer and two packs of cigarettes. I woke up Thanksgiving morning in a completely vacant lot. I swear there was only a burrito wrapper blowing down the aisle. The colorful barns were now huge barren metal sheds the size of football fields. And I was alone...with five tired horses.

Clayton arrived late that evening and congratulated me on making it through. "That Sarah's a piece of work, ain't she?" he sorta asked himself. Well that was the end of the season. "I pretty much take care of things at home myself over the winter," he added. "But I'm sure you'll find more work soon. Sarah says you're good with the horses"

He then added, "I hear there is a big league Grand Prix dressage rider training at Santa Fe's 7500 foot altitudes with those big Hanoverian horses. She's looking for a real show groom. Look her up when you get back to town."

I was about to discover the difference between the Velvet heads and the Dressage Nazis.

Not too long ago, I heard from someone that Amanda had become a crack addict and posed for Playboy or some stupid stuff. As for Katie, I prayed Katie married into more money and bought M&M.

El Tigre

I drove into Galisteo Creek Ranch in the La Cienega foothills of Santa Fe and I felt exhilarated. Emily's mom had let me see her for a whole day, which sort of made up for a whole year, for me anyway. I was in better spirits after a successful string of shows that summer. I felt like I was good at what I was doing and available to keep doing it.

As I walked into the beautiful stable I was met by a friendly barn worker, Manuel, who shook my hand and pointed me towards the grand indoor riding arena behind the barn. I entered and saw a red-faced woman, struggling up/down, up/down, trying to pace herself with the horse which looked like a struggle for her.

A strong California girl type woman was sitting in the bleachers with a cell phone in her hand. She shouted commands into a wireless headphone set which the rider was also wearing with a helmet.

I watched for awhile trying to figure out what they were doing. “Heels down. Shoulders back. Toes in. Push, push. No. With your hips.” I could already tell this girl got paid to yell at older, richer women. The instructor, wearing dirty riding pants and old nasty boots that looked like she lived in them, extended her hand. “Joanie Bolton. What can I do for you?”

“Really?” I said with a firm business like handshake. "I'm Britt Darby...I’ve been...”

“Yeah. Caroline told me everything about you. I heard you were good with really bad horses,” she declared. “Well I’ve got some naughty ones. Smart, talented, but naughty.”

She had a steady stream of students, mostly older, richer, whiter customers than I had ever seen before. She also needed a groom and there I was, just for her, since I had nothing else better to do with my life. There was a garage attached to the barn where I could put the van and construct somewhat of a makeshift apartment.

Breakfast would be served at six . Manuel covered that and most everything else. I would just be saddling up student’s horses, to be ready when they arrived to be yelled at, one after the other - paying to be told what they were doing wrong.

All afternoon I'd be giving baths and cleaning tack. It was a wonderful set up, with 15 large stalls in a semi-circle around a courtyard with a fountain and a large grooming area. My own office.

The tack room was filled with a load of expensive looking polished saddles, which were now in my care, as well as bridles. The bridles had way more control looking features including nose bands, two bits, and two sets of reins. There were also a lot of polo leg protectors - leg wraps to protect the horse from walking all over himself.

The level of horses was certainly a step up. The dressage horses, especially the German Hanoverians, were magnificent. Brilliant, bigger and badder than anything I'd seen. Some sort of super-uber-equine. Rhinos raised in Bavaria, probably left by the Romans on their way to the North Pole or Bethlehem or the Olympics.

They were different from the sleek jumpers and the rib-thin racers. The financial factor was bigger too. Some of these creatures went for $300,000 or more and Joanie was in the business to be sure. She could ride like nothing I'd ever seen, even in the movies. She sat effortlessly on any horse, in any situation it seemed. Shoulders strong, impeccable balance, relaying instructions through the saddle with no visible cues to the onlooker. Even during bucking bouts she remained unmovable from her commanding seat. I assumed even the toughest rodeo bronc rider could learn a thing or two from Joanie Bolton - or at least pay to get yelled at.

The first of her babies was "Wizard", an incredible, delectable, little/big Dustin Hoffman kind of goofy, expensive, 1400 lbs. baby. A huge dark silly bay of who she said, "His mind is impeccable. His manners are not." Perhaps I might do something with him. He was easily distracted, handsome and fearless. He had a certain way of ignoring you, even when being fed. This horse needed serious attitude adjustment and I was just the clown to do it. He was "trying to be four". She said he'd just be competing in Level 1 this season. She informed me a Grand Prix horse took ten or more years to ascend to the top level. He had the family line, size ,and confirmation of a great horse.

Her second pupil, Nikita was very similar in appearance to "Wiz", only bigger, badder, and afraid of everything - wide eyed, on the edge, always nervous and freaky. Both were "gifted" she assured me. "They just need some work."

Joanie spent a lot of time on the phone negotiating buying deals and, along with clinics that she gave occasionally out-of-state, and shows, there were endless schedules to re-shuffle. She also had a serious habit of misplacing her sunglasses, gloves, whips, money, etc., which I soon found to be part of the job...Keeping track of Joanie, for Joanie. Like a rockstar, only it was the horses who were on the drugs.

Things went smoothly that winter. I had known three of her students before from Tesuque: Luann with Rosella, her huge well-schooled ride and Linda Love and her daughter, Olivia neutron-bomb, who kind of shared Malcolm. The mother/daughter factor always seemed to rear its ugly head. Believe me, Caroline and Sarah provided more heated moments than I had time to waste on in this book.

I actually managed to get Wiz and Niki in my pocket rather quickly. They loved me. I didn't ask them to do anything. I didn't ride them. I didn't yell at them. I had learned hissing worked well and speaking in German, "Nein. Nien." I brushed and cuddled them, kept the flies off them, and after a brutal lesson, I would whisk them away from the tyrant, give them a bath, rub their legs down, and massage their backs before putting their pajamas on and tucking them in for dinner. I would kneel at rope's end with a cigarette as they chomped on the grass in the front breezeway.

El Tigre

Our first show was the Spring Classic in Parker, Colorado. There was a relatively small band going - "four horses and the three Tesuque girls." Their husbands were bankrolling the tour. I completely understand that most civilians have no idea that there are people in the world who, as we speak, are just sitting around under Cizano umbrellas while their Mexicans scurry about the RV's, rows of Mercedes, and golf carts, playing with horses. But there are.

The Colorado Horse Park was a spectacular setting in the mountains - flags waving in the spring breezes, colorful tents with venders of tack, horse supplies, fancy riding attire, food stops, and grandstands with a lush polo field to graze the horses after a ride. There were rows of huge barns with as many as five hundred horses bustling in the fair-like atmosphere. We unloaded the tack trunks and racks of formal riding clothes, quickly filling the stalls with eight bags of shavings per horse. Then we unloaded the horses. First Rosella, at 18 hands high, - huge. She was also an import from Germany. Very well trained, very well behaved. Then Malcolm, poor Malcolm (long story). He was an ex-racehorse and it showed.

Wiz came off the trailer like a clumsy cow on the way to the slaughter and Niki came off, totally freaked out as usual.

"Put everything where it's supposed to be then take him for a long walk. Show him everything and don't come back 'til he's calmed down. We're going back to the hotel. If there's any problems, call me."

I handed Joanie her phone, sunglasses, wallet, and truck keys from my pants pocket.

Rockets on a Rope

Now something very wonderful happened, finally, as I was filling waters. Emily, Melissa and John came walking down the aisle. "Daddy!!" I couldn't believe my eyes. "Wow."

They were on the way to Denver for a one night visit to John's family and Emily had seen the sign on the highway to the show. They'd talked about having her spend the night with me, "if she could?" Unbelievably, I really was in heaven. Tomorrow was an easy warm-up day, plus Galisteo Creek had a trailer with a small apartment in it. I still slept in a stall with the troop but I would make an exception tonight! This was going to be a show to remember. "Wow, this is pretty cool," John stated as they left. I couldn't agree more.

I needed to get Niki out before he melted down. So Emily followed at a safe distance away. She was seven at this time. Niki trotted sideways and Emily laughed when he snorted, which he did often, warily eyeing all the new sights and distractions with us.

I put him away, now acquainted with his new surroundings. Emily was hungry, so we fired up the golf cart and drove down to the burrito bus. After we ate, I spent the sunset hours teaching her to drive the cart. She was great at it, a very good driver. It was a blast. We did donuts and cruised around the place at full speed and we laughed like I hadn't in years, honestly.

We bunked down early on the bed in the trailer, parked a half-mile from the barns down by the showers. I awoke that day at 5 a.m. to the sound of my daughter breathing beautifully, laying next to me. I snuck out, leaving the golf cart keys and a note reminding her how to find our barn.

El Tigre

The look on her proud face, as she drove up alone. She looked so big all of a sudden. As I attended to morning chores, she watched me muck the first stall, a little bored and unimpressed by what I did for a living. Luckily, Linda and Olivia showed up first and while her mom rode Malcolm, Olivia offered to ride around with Emily in the cart, picking up a few supplies and strawberry slushies!

By the time Joanie arrived, so did Melissa and John. They wanted to stick around to see the event but needed to get back to Santa Fe. Emily was actually way more into the golf cart and not so much the horses, but it had been an incredible breath of fresh air for me.

So, after a long hug that I will never forget and hope Emily doesn't either, I watched her walk away, again. And went back to work.

Now the horses know when you're drunk or hurt or both and that night I was all of the above. I had had such a wonderful time with Emily Grace but it also made me painfully aware of how much I was missing out on her life. Niki sniffed my pants with his head down low and then nuzzled me as I put on his evening blanket. Most of the white folk had disappeared by now and a handful of Mexicans were closing down shop.

I went out front for a smoke as a groom across the way held up a beer and offered, "Some serious looking horses, Senior."

I walked over and introduced myself.

"Are they your wives?" he asked.

"No, I'm the groom," I replied laughing.

"Really?" he pondered and laughed.

After a few too many, swapping sad stories about our patrons and children, I bid Ramon good night. I was kind of startled by how the dressage grooms were better with English and looked a lot more "well kept" than the jumping beans I was used to. I sort of stumbled back to the barn for last call and not seeing Wiz, I looked in his stall, to find him laying down in the fluffy shavings. I slid the door open slightly and snuck in and sat down between his two front legs, under his big head and began stroking his neck. He didn't move. He just heaved a tired sigh and I passed out.

About 5 a.m. I was startled awake by the horse struggling to stand up around me. We had both slept through the night like that. I crawled out into the aisle. "Hhhmmm." No music. I needed to get a radio. I went out for a morning wake-up smoke and wondered exactly how many people had really slept with a horse? I figured probably just the old west cowboys and the Romans. I got on with the morning ritual. Joanie was not amused when I suggested to her I'd been in all night with the Wiz.

"Were you drunk?"

"Of course. But what does that have to do with it? I'm like a god to them!!"

She walked towards the tack room and said, "Saddle up Messiah."

Joanie and I were secretly in love too. She left me alone with the horses and I didn't tell her how to ride. Much cooler than my other gigs, I actually went with her anywhere, anytime there was a horse involved. Like Elvis, she was a star in the dressage spotlight, competing and doing well in the Pan-American Games, pictures in magazines, high-dollar clients, etc. etc.

I'd walk the horse briskly while she followed ten paces behind on the cell phone. I'd toss her on the horse and she'd hand me her phone, glasses, and spit the gum out. I'd hand her the crop and gloves, remove the horses warm-up leggings and pick his hooves one last time, then lean on a fence with a cigarette and watch them go round in dramatic circles.

I felt like a more active part of the ride. I began to figure out what it was they were doing and even what it was supposed to look like. I knew enough to tell the good from the poor, even if I didn't know exactly what was going on. I didn't want to know how to ride. I liked where I was, with the horses, one on one on the ground, in the herd. On top of that I could sense I had a gift, a bond, a respect, for these magnificent beings that had literally and physically built this country and won the wars but had now become a hobby - an expensive hobby.

All of our horses did surprisingly well the first day. Nobody was expected to win (except Luann) and no matter how great of a rider Joanie was, her horses were young and silly and naughty, as such. They just needed the show experience more than anything. I was proud Joanie acknowledged my involvement in the process. Not only was I precise, on time, self-motivated and confident, the horses responded to the security I provided.

Ms. Bolton had commented that Niki's back seemed sore and he was "twitchin'" a bit under the saddle. She said he seemed uncomfortable, but was trying to be "cooperative."

Wizard had just been "the wiz". He had a goofy twist to him that gave you the impression that he didn't take this discipline stuff too seriously and he was big enough to get away with it he thought. Olivia complained that Malcolm was "lazy and unresponsive" due to how her mother rode him. As usual, the 14 year-old girls were better riders than the parents, probably due to better lessons, better horses, better everything than their moms had had way back when. Luann, though not a tremendous jockey, always won her amateur class because, basically, she just had more horse than anyone else. At any level, Rosella always looked good.

A new additive to my evenings were the braiders, nymphs that came in during the night, roaming the cavernous barns, tying the horses manes into even shorter knots in tedious corn rows that added to the high class appearance of Dressage. They were usually paid $75 per head and went from horse to horse an hour or two per, depending on "attitude." They rarely knew the clients and stood precariously on step-stools.

Under next to unknown odds, I had learned to meticulously pick the tiny braids out after a ride with a sewing stitch needle, trying never to clip a stray hair or risk being punished by one of these ladies of the night. I discovered the horses didn't like them as much as the spectators - the braids, that is.

As I put Niki away for the night, I reached out to brush something off his withers. He flinched, shuddering. I pulled away, stood and looked at him standing a little crooked in the stall. I held my hand back up flat as if to say "peace" and, when I was an inch or so away, his withers shivered again as long as I held my hand there. When

I backed away he stopped, then repeated to shake his whole body and snort at me.

I ran my two fingers along his spinal cord and he arched his back inward as though I was poking him. This "wasn't good" as Stuart would say. As I reached back for his withers, he snapped with his teeth at me. I left him alone.

That night, around 3:30 a.m., Kat the braider showed up looking sleepy, worn out, and in a hurry. She started with Wiz as I came out of his stall and went to check on Niki. Niki was laying down. I asked Kat how it was going. She'd had some screwballs in the last barn and was running late. As she completed Wiz, I told her, "Just get the other two. Don't worry about Niki. He's not going anywhere." I'd never seen a horse do that. I knew it wasn't colic and I would explain that to J.B. in the morning.

That was easier said than done, as Niki's stall was the first she came to that morning.

Joanie looked in and bellowed, "Britt, why aren't his braids in?"

"Is he still laying down?" I responded, "Yes. He's hurt. I don't think you should ride him today."

"Well, that's not your decision to make now, is it?"

"Well, you're paying me to look after them and I'm not here to baby sit your ego. So I say he's hurt."

"Go get my saddle and shut up. And give him some goddamned Bute!"

I'd done that already. She crazily tied some tennis-shoe string bows in his mane and placed the saddle on as he sagged beneath it. Niki stood at quivering attention. She paused. I went on back to my mucking. From the stall I was in, I heard a rustling, a stirring, a couple of snorts, followed by what sounded like somebody hitting the dirt... Hard.

I came out to find, for probably the first time on earth, Joan Bolton, ladies and gentleman, Joan Bolton - sprawled on the floor, calling the vet. Niki trotted out the door.

"He's hurt," she deduced. "Go get him. Put him away and get Wizard ready."

Finding Niki was not hard. He'd stopped just out front, waiting for me. We had a cigarette together. I put him back, put his blankets back on, and kissed him goodbye. I went and got Wizard, who pulled in a shocking second place. That left me the afternoon to run to the Walmart and pick up bottled water, other supplies, and a radio.

While I was gone Joanie had called an old semi-retired Olympic vet, Danny Marks, who was doing Acupuncture nowadays and was at the show. She assured me she could handle everything and sent me on my way.

"No beer," she yelled.

"Yeah, right," I yelled back. "Whiskey for everyone."

When I returned an hour later, Nikita lay sprawled on the barn floor - Dead. It turned out that while having a six-inch needle placed in his sciatic nerve he freaked out, reared up, and fell over into a stall wall, breaking his shoulder and possibly his neck. They'd put him down on the spot.

"Jesus! Why didn't you wait for me?" I screamed as I knelt beside my quiet friend.

Immediately, the truck drove up to haul away the $300,000 dollar carcass.

"God, Joanie. What the hell am I here for?"

I went back to my stall and sat and cried for an hour. Everyone left the barn quickly that afternoon in shocked silence.

Joanie said we'd do Wizards last class in the morning because he needed the points to continue through the summer shows. Then we'd head back to Santa Fe early. No one was in the mood to ride. Wiz didn't do well. I don't think Joanie was necessarily with the program either. After performing a second rate act, he leapt completely out of the ring and then back in again to wind it up! The judges comment on the back of the card said, "Nice Exit." We loaded the remaining three up, took off and just south of Raton, Joanie got on her phone and sold Wizard on the spot, to some hunter/jumper farm in California, where she said he'd probably do better with less discipline and more free rein. I couldn't believe it. I needed a break from horses, but mostly horse people.

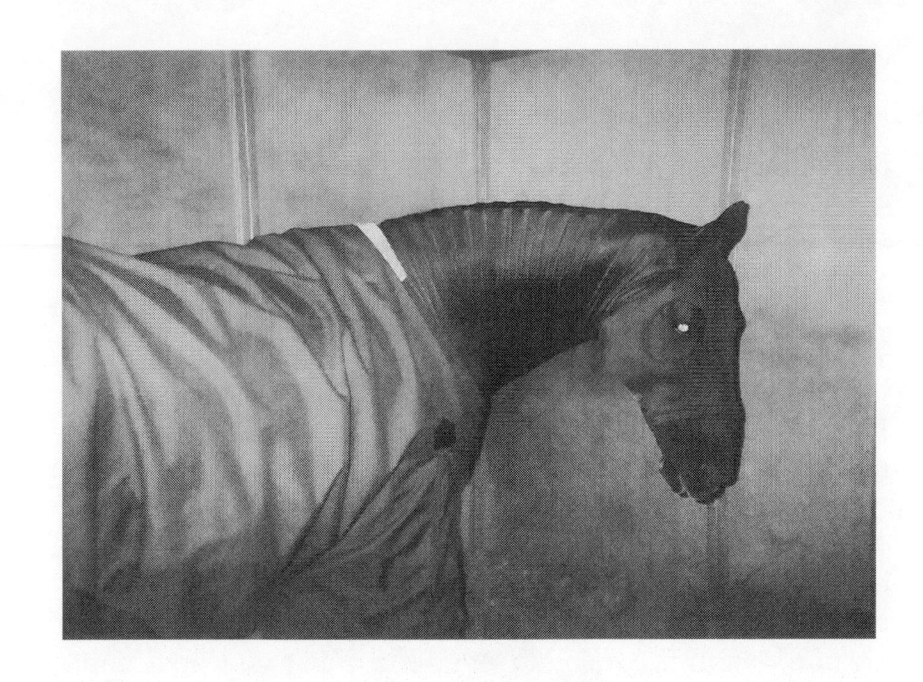

Mazarin

When I lived in Tesuque, I had mucked a small one-horse corral for a woman named Margaret. Her husband Michael reproduced antique Indian motorcycle parts in an incredible manufacturing shop in his home. From lost wax molds to chromoly steel kick stands, brake levers and luggage racks - you name it - all the parts the hippies had lost in the 60's. Authentic. Quality stuff. It was a very lucrative small market deal. He needed sandblasting and grinding done and right now nothing sounded better than rolling red-hot steel in my hands, which were actually starting to look and feel the wear.

I had bid Joanie "adios" and had been camping out at unknown locations in the hills for a few months. While working for Michael, I had become extremely skilled in the art of grinding, shaping and polishing motorcycle parts.

Rockets on a Rope

One day, to my surprise, my daughter's mother comes up to one of my secret hide-outs to inform me, "Joan Bolton is trying to get hold of you. She sounds frantic."

She *is* frantic," I said. "Thanks Melissa... for whatever, forever."

I reluctantly walked down to Andreas' pay phone and inquired as to her predicament.

"Hey Britt."

I heard the familiar "Phoney" Joanie I had heard when I overheard her sell a halfway descent prospect to an unsuspecting buyer.

" I've got the horse, I swear. This is my Grand Prix ticket, I'm sure this is my shot at the Olympics."

I didn't know they had dressage in the Olympics, but they do. Jumping too. Athens 2004 was next summer.

Was she kidding me? What part of "I really can't stand you" hadn't she heard?

"I know we've had our disagreements from time to time," she continued, "but we work well together and this is the right horse for you too. You're the best groom I've ever had. You know what you're doing and the horses love you a lot."

Well that was certainly thoughtful.

"This one's a little hot, well, a handful and pretty darn big...ah, well, 18 hands. As big as Rosella but a hell of a lot more horsepower... He's a Hanoverian stallion. He'll love you. I love you. You'll love it."

Rockets on a Rope

Love was the last thing on my mind.

When was the show?

"Tomorrow... I'll pick you up at 5 a.m. Manuel can pack the trailer."

Well, shoot! If Manuel was helping out, I told her I'd have to get paid cash on the barrelhead, as much as I'd get with a full school of students. I told her I'd really rather not talk with her or deal with her much and if she just left the two of us alone and just showed up for the ride and used a mounting block instead of my back.

We met in the Tesuque church parking lot at 5 a.m. I jumped in without looking in the back of the rocking trailer. I showed her that I had brought my Boy Scout pack, just in case.

On the drive to Parker she explained the history of this horse. He'd competed and done well when he was younger in Germany and Switzerland. Then he'd ended up at a stud farm in Idaho, running loose, like Rising Star, until his mane and tail were full of burrs. He was traded to an older couple in Truth or Consequences for a bunch of babies. They had brought him to Joanie after seeing her name in a magazine in an ad for saddles.

He was a brilliant horse, Joanie had concluded - and she knew horses. He was just a little rough around the edges... Just my cup of tea. He clearly knew what he was doing. He just needed to be reminded of how to behave. Now taking an eighteen hand stallion to a dressage show is a lot like trying to do your algebra homework - at a strip club.

Mazarin

As we pulled up to the barn, the pounding on the inner walls of the trailer and the lion-like screams bellowing from inside led me to believe this could be a circus and it promised to be a different kind of show all together.

The come-hither-to whinnies of the excited mares in waiting, already in the barns, led him to believe he was back at the Love Ranch. Joanie slid open the front window of the empty seven-horse trailer and tried to put a chain over his nose with an extra-long leather lead rope.

“Ok,” she said. “We won’t go in there with him. You just let me know when you’re ready and I’ll release him up here after you open the back door.”
I wasn’t really convinced that sounded like a plan.

“Just make sure you catch him on his way out!”

That didn’t sound like the greatest idea, but I agreed to “On 1,2,3!!!"

Coming at me at about a hundred miles an hour was a blur from the darkest depths of the trailer, the biggest chestnut butt I'd ever seen. Shaking the trailer, he pounded his way back. Several people stood by watching the commotion.

I held my arm up high in the air... not really too clear on what exactly I was reaching for. He leapt out of the trailer and paused for a split second. I grabbed hold of the leather lead, right where it meets the end of the chain, and clamped my hands down. He slammed his left shoulder into mine, as we spun around, and took off with a jump past the startled crowd. "You can go home now. The show’s over,” I yelled as we rumbled down the barn row.

At this point I couldn't even tell what he looked like and I was using all that I had learned at the racetrack to push him toward his stall. Slamming the door shut tight, he reared up and screamed loudly, announcing he had arrived. Joanie walked up laughing, "He's spunky, huh?" I stood and stared, quite possibly facing death itself on four legs - Mazarin...

There had been a strain of West Nile Virus in the Southwest that summer so the promoters had spread the competition out, more than usual. Since we had no students and because he was screaming and pounding and actually trying to climb over the ten foot high stall walls, we ended up alone at our end of the barn. Perfect. Just me and Maz side by side in hell. The West Nile had added a new feature to the winning equation - activity all night., trucks coming and going, and vets and upset owners prowling the aisles. Pretty much lights on constantly - like the racetrack, only fancier.

With only one horse, mucking had become a twenty-four hour a day job. I fed him the exact amount of food every meal. He pooped exactly twelve times a day if all was going well and I picked them up within fifteen seconds after he delivered, as I was staying on top of things. He peed in the exact same spot, directly in the center of the stall. I never had to use the extra bags of shavings that were now my fort. He never laid down because of all the distractions and the stall was fluffy and fresh throughout the whole ordeal.

I had a lot of time to stand around and smoke. I had learned not to hang out with the other grooms. The party was over. I drank my beer alone, sort of. I threw one in Maz's grain each evening also. German horse, German beer. We were big time. One horse, one groom. One rider, one goal. We didn't come here to lose.

He looked a little droopy that morning as we awoke to the sound of the classical music station that seemed to help take his mind off things. I assumed it was the lack of sleep or the beer or... Oh, holy mother of Tesuque! He was a snuggle bunny!

I'd been up this trail before. The fire breather I'd escorted off the trailer the night before was apparently bipolar. It wasn't West Nile Virus. I'd seen that already. He was a victim of the "way too big of a horse" syndrome. Everyone was afraid of him, even hated him, so he just played along. He was a son of a bitch on stage and a lush on the couch at home. He was lonely, inside and out. "Welcome to the Club, Mr. Mazarin. Shall we begin with a walk?"

He was covered from head to toe in an army green, spandex body-glove called a "sleezy", high-tech long underwear. Slim would love it. On top of that, a lightweight evening jacket...Real sporty! It did make it easier to keep him spotless after rolling around in sixteen inches of shavings.

This also explains why I wasn't even sure what color he was during the dance we had had the night before. I peeled the spandex face mask off which had previously only revealed his nose, mouth and deep eyes. A huge square chestnut skull appeared with set of big brown eyes that looked an awful lot like Bambi's.

"What's up, buttercup?" I asked as I reached for his hay-filled water bucket. "Rough night, kitten?" He seemed intrigued. I picked up his feet and picked out the dirt from the road. He stood like a trained show dog as I brushed him out and sprayed a show sheen/fly spray mix on. I smoothed his ears, cleaned his eyes, wiped his nose, bent down and nibbled on his nostril. Then blew a steady breeze of cigarette smoke in his face and turned away and peed on his spot. I believe he thought I was his mother.

I now had my own cell phone that Joanie had provided. She called and said she wasn't even coming over today. It was only warm-ups and she didn't have to warm-up. So we were free to spend the day as we liked.

"How's it going?" she asked.

"Great," I confidently spoke.

"Really?"

"Yeah, sure. He's a piece of cake. No problemo. See you manana. Over and out."

I put my cell back in my pocket and pulled out a carrot. He smelled it, acted like he didn't know what it was and like he still didn't trust me, so I put it back in my pants and left to go get his protective leg boots, halter, and chain. As I walked back, dangling the silver lead chain, he woke up. Totally show time, Elvis.

It was a bit of a struggle getting the halter on the first time. He was a big asshole and he knew it. Kind of like Kilmer, although without the bad acting. He pranced sideways and snorted as we descended down the barn entrance. He was a lot to hold on to and he knew it. We basically high-stepped at a fast clip that he set, moving ahead of me a step or two. We tried to get as far away from the mares as quickly as possible, or at least that's what I was trying to do.

Mazarin

Getting out onto the polo field grasses, he finally relaxed after giving one last shout out back to the mares in the barn, as if to say, "I'm over here if you need me." Then he seriously went about pulling some grass up as I knelt down and had a smoke. "Tough life, huh, superstar?" He blew out his quivering nostrils and looked me squarely in the eyes as if to say he agreed.

I decided I'd better sweep the place, like Emily and I had done with Nikita, so we knew our way around. He was a sight to see, dancing and blowing all the way around the facility. Pulling me when other horses were close by, yet in a Siamese Twin sort of way, staying with me. He was working with me.

He'd actually built up quite a sweat by then just showing off, so I figured we'd cruise on down to the showers and wrap this thing up early. As we galloped up to the wash rack there were quite a few other boys with their ponies and quite a few of them moved further down as we approached. I noticed a younger hito in a hunter/jumper t-shirt and figured he'd apparently come over to the dark side too.

With the lead rope in my left hand, a cigarette in my mouth, and the hose in my right hand, I began to spray the hot horse down. As he reared up, kicking his front hooves like Trigger, I sprayed his belly down, then blasted his private parts 'til he stood back down like a proper gentleman. I'd learned that from Ariana many moons ago. I said "Thank you, kind sir" as I soaked his face off.

At that point the young lad walked over to us and innocently inquired, "Are you the one they call El Tigre? The Great White Groom?" I squinted at him like I thought Clint Eastwood would have as he continued. "I have heard tales of a primo, primo who can drink more beer than any man, yet still muck like the wind and always has the finest horses."

I looked at Maz, then back at the kid again. I could swear I could hear that whistling harmonica song from the spaghetti westerns. "Oh, yeah. Sure, José. That's me. Have you seen Je'sus? Or been to a cantina anywheres close by?" I gestured for him to shut off the water.

"What's your name, by the way?" I added.

"José," he responded. "Good guess...Que?" He pondered.

"Don't worry about it. Who's got the bud?"

He smiled and ran off, apparently satisfied with my response. Wow, I'd finally made it big. I was famous for digging shit. I felt like calling my mom and dad. I felt like I was 33 again.

This was the *Dressage in the Rockies Championships*, the year-end finale. Both of us were sleeping better. He was getting two brews with dinner. Joanie actually thought it was a pretty good idea! And it saved money on the Banamine bill. Maz was starting to receive routine Cortisone injections in his aging hocks and front feet from by the aforementioned needle king. I was living on Mountain Dew and smoke.

Joanie's ride wasn't until 1 o'clock in the afternoon. We had agreed she wouldn't arrive 'til high noon and a half. Her car pulled up just as I finished polishing him off with a toxic blend of fly poison, baby oil and Miracle Groom, that I'd found made them less shiny and more real and in Maz's case, perfect. I precisely positioned the crisp white pad and $7000 saddle on his broad back and clamped up the cinch as he wiggled.

He truly was a “rocket on a rope” as I assertively bridled him up that morning, after squirting water in his mouth with a syringe to remove any trace of hay or grain. He had kicked on full-engines as Joanie walked in the barn. She wanted to be sure everything was just right and it was. Timing, they say, is everything.

“He’s a lot better than he is at home,” she said as I crushed the nose band onto his furry head using Redford’s clippers until it was part of his skin. “Power Steering,” she called it. “I’m a genius!” I exclaimed, as I finished my masterpiece, to no response. Joanie went to get on her monkey hat as I walked him up and down the aisle. “Alright Man O’ War. Let’s go get them.”

Watching the ride, for the first time really seeing Grand Prix level “Prix St. George” Dressage performed correctly and properly, was breathtaking to say the least. The power, the grace apparent, the two of them seemingly one, executing military maneuvers like the Spanish school of riding. Going from one end of the arena to the other in a grand ballet of flying changes. The scores would not be posted until late in the afternoon. I handed her a bottle of water as she slid off and simply stated, "That worked!"

I quickly trotted away with Maz. Joanie stayed behind to soak up congratulations and the admiration of the crowd that had gathered. Arriving at the showers to the whoops, whistles, and cries of all the primos, I had a sure feeling we had won and a strange feeling we’d won more than just Dressage in the Rockies.

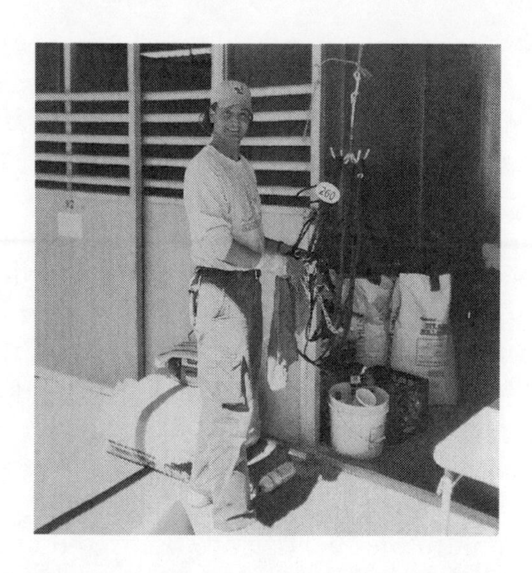

The 4H County Fair

As I was graining Maz and adding two beers to his bucket, Joanie came walking down the aisle with a stern, serious, inner reflection, kind of look. "There," she said, throwing a baseball hat at me that bounced off the stall door and into the dirt. "I picked that up for you."

I shut the door and picked up the cap from the floor as she kept going into the tack room. I looked at the writing on the front: "Dressage in the Rockies F.E.I. High Points Champion." On the back, where you adjust it to fit, it read: "First Place, Best of Show. Now, I had no idea who the F.E.I were but I was certainly glad they didn't test for drugs.

It turned out the judge that day was an Olympic judge whose name was Jane Ayers. She had given my two trained monkeys some score that meant something and we'd gotten a blue ribbon to prove it. That score had been cosmically posted through some modern computer world-wide dressage deal and we'd come up twelfth in the world that day, which qualified us for the Olympic trials in Del Mar, California next spring. From the tack room office, I could hear a little girl on a cell phone call to her parents laughing and crying at once. I went out front for a smoke.

I began to load up the trailer late that afternoon. Joanie had actually done some interviews with *Chronicle of the Horse* and some internet news crap that slowed us down. Dark clouds loomed in the west. I strung a long lunge line with a chain on the end. The line stretched from my drivers side window back to the front window of the trailer. This involved duct-taping a one-inch piece of PVC plastic tubing inside the window, then taping the window shut, so I could run the chain through to bonehead and pull on him like a riverboat captain when he kicked at the stop lights, which was inevitably adding to his foot problems.

"Britt. You're a genius," Joanie finally figured out. She then suggested, "Why don't you go to the public bathrooms and take a shower, for me? For the ride home please?" I hated it when she tried to be nice. And I had learned a long time ago that horses were herd animals and I was part of the herd. They relied on scent for identification and social status and since I was basically living in shit 24/7, it never really made sense to clean up in a formal way. I was cute in Hollywood and talented but it doesn't really matter. Like Sarah used to say, "This isn't a beauty contest." Besides, I liked living on the dirty side.

My compadres in Tucson had taught me to put Mane & Tail shampoo under my hat. Then when you took your horse to the showers, it would seep down and you could either spray yourself off or a playful primo would do it for you. I had actually brought a pair of dirty pants from a previous show for when I met Maz for the first time, just to let him know I was serious.

Rockets on a Rope

I grudgingly ran to the showers with the impending storm hanging above. As I turned on the hot water it began to hail. Then the bathroom door blew open...No. It blew off! Nearby flashes of lightning and immediate thunder then exploded, as the storm was right on top of us. I threw my clothes back on, running to the barn. Portable toilets were laying face down. Half the roof of at least part of one barn ripped upward like a tuna can. Streams of slushy ice-white mud flowed everywhere.

Joanie was standing by Maz's stall door feeding him carrots. "I wish you would have gotten him on the trailer before this,"

"Yeah, well ,whatever."

I was astonished, or maybe not. We sat in the barn aisle in silence. As much as there can be silence at a horse show, in a tornado... I mean there was no phone reception at this time.

A few soaking wet riders came in from somewhere and the horses' tails were sticking straight up in the air. Lightning had struck at least one horse and rider in a warm-up ring and quite a few had been knocked clean off their mounts. This was starting to look like a jumper show. When the wind and rain had slowed down to a drizzle, I led the victorious stallion to the waiting limo. We were late starting the eight-hour drive back to Santa Fe and I was incredibly wired on Mountain Dew. The first time Maz kicked as we pulled up to a stop sign, I tugged on the line like a steamship whistle and we took off down the road, all quiet. That worked!

Joanie began to explain we had qualified for the Olympic trials. We were on some sort of a "short list" and there were no more serious shows until Del Mar, California. She had decided taking our star pupil to the year-end County Fair show in Albuquerque would be a good way to keep his head in the game.

His Cortisone treatments would continue through the winter, as some X-rays had shown a tiny chip in his front right foot. Mazarin was seventeen years old. We pulled out of a gas stop on the highway south of Raton. Joanie had bought me a pack of Camels and we shared a bottle of wine as we drove through Las Vegas, New Mexico, where it's not legal to drink and drive, but it's common and accepted, according to Kilmer.

I awoke the first morning of the Albuquerque show with six inches of snow drifting through the old wooden planks of the nasty outdoor accommodations of the State Fair racetrack with my half-million dollar horse. All the students had also come. This was a schooling show and I was back to power mucking and dragging slop-filled carts through a slushy mess, like some Dickens character. Oh, yeah. This was a splendid idea.

In the stall adjacent to ours, the father of one of the enemy riders watched curiously as I spoke to Mazarin every time I'd pass by. "This sucks secretariat," I smirked at one point, receiving a silly whinny and a curling of the lips high in the air.

"Who are you guys?" he called out, eyeing the picks and rags and bottles hanging from my mud soaked uniform.

"Oh, just a Girl Scout troop from Santa Fe," I said sarcastically.

"No. I mean, who are you two?" He pointed to the big horse. "And who's your rider?" My daughter claims she just read something about her in some magazine. Joan somebody?"

"Oh, yeah?" I said. "I guess she's somebody!"

"This is a kids show!" he retorted.

"Actually it's a 'schooling show," I corrected him and responded,"We're 'schooling'!"

"My Samantha's worked hard for this all year and I've spent a fortune on show sheen."

I looked at Maz,, who I wasn't even dusting off at this point, since there wasn't any dust and what was the point?

"And you're competing against us? How does that work?"

"Look, dad," I politely informed him. "Our saddles cost more than your horse. My horse costs more than your house. We're the twelfth ranked ride in the world and if it's any consolation, we probably won't be trying too hard. Would ya like a cold one?"

Mazarin kicked on the stall door and farted.

My rider arrived and we went to work. I drug my muddy, wet hero through the muck up to the indoor arena with Joanie on board, on the cell phone. She talked right up until the judge signaled her entrance and she threw me the thing as she rode in, much to the delight of all the squealing little girls in the spectator seats, along with Doubting Thomas, or "Dear ol' Dad", as I liked to call him.

We won, hopefully, unless Samantha had some surprises up her $140 sleeve. I packed the mess up to return to Santa Fe and felt like Don Diego De Vargas! I saw dad across the road, throwing some hay to his child's Second Place finisher.

I grabbed the blue ribbon off the top of Joanie's tack trunk and sloshed it over to him. "There you go, dad," I said, "That's what it's all about right there. Your daughter deserves it and so do you." He gave me a hug. I was missing Emily spiritually and was glad the show was over.
A few weeks later the trip to California was a familiar one. Passing by the Flagstaff rodeo grounds, I rolled down the truck window and hung out, whistling, "Ese' primo! See you at the next show."

Driving through the Mojave desert, I vaguely remembered my Hollywood daze and driving back to Iowa for the holidays. Arriving in San Diego, I was startled by the traffic and congestion, probably from too much time living in stalls and in the mountains, free from any city for years.

We unloaded Maz. I was having to go drag him out by now. Joanie said matter of factly that his bone chip was causing some "problems" but he was getting something like $10,000 worth of shots tomorrow, so everything would be just dandy. As I walked him to his stall he leaned on me in a pretty pathetic way, more than he ever had in the past.

We were in the Del Mar stables of Gunter Siedel, one of the top riders on the world stage, and a business associate of Joanie. The barn was incredible, complete with ten yard long Jacuzzi pools for the horses. Mexican boys came with feather dusters, cleaning the stall door bars off. A palm tree lined cool-down path led out to the Pacific ocean beach.

He was hurt, I could tell, as we strolled down along the waves that first afternoon. Smoking a cigarette, we pondered the universe. Suddenly a large military-style jeep appeared. Driving was a fat beach patrol idiot who informed me I had to put the cigarette out! "It's his. I'm just holding it for him." (No response.) I pointed towards the city and close by Tijuana and stated, "I don't think I'm the problem here." He obviously had no sense of humor. We went back to the beautiful barn, extinguished.

After Joanie went back to her hotel, I went for the last supper. I looked in to see Maz kind of standing sideways on three legs, favoring his front right foot. I sat down in his stall against the wall and got blasted.

I called Joanie around midnight-thirty, a.m., p.m., whatever, and responded to her groggy, "What is it?" with, "It's over. That's what it is, you jerk. I'm sick of your shit. Why did you push him all winter? What the hell is all this Cortisone gonna do? It's over. I quit, I'm out of here."

By morning I had loaded up my backpack with my two pairs of pants and twenty pairs of socks and told my stunned boss, "He's hurt. You're not riding him and I'm not sticking around to watch if you think you are." I was taking the train back to Santa Fe. "There are other people here who can take care of him," I suggested half-heartedly. "You're fine. You're the expert. You can deal with things on your own."

I hitchhiked to La Jolla on the way to the train station and, sitting by the beach where we'd had our sushi barbecue, I thought of John Jr. who crashed his plane into the ocean and the homeless guy who might have had "it" figured out.

I realized that probably the only real thing I knew for sure in this life was how to defend myself verbally. And I know I've mentioned a lot of names in this book, but in the long run the biggest one I ever dropped was Mazarin.

The 4H County Fair

Upon returning home, I was informed I wouldn't be attending Emily's birthday, as Melissa's "next new" boyfriend Michael "didn't want me around." After a quick call to reveal my feelings about the situation, instead of waiting around for the incoming restraining order which was on it's way, I was back on my way to Iowa again in my Dad's '75 Chevy van, without an Olympic Medal or blue ribbon, or whatever it is you get.

Reedannland

It wasn't racing season in the chilly Midwest, so I began to scout out some mom and pop barns in the area around Des Moines. I received a call one afternoon from Dr. Alan Ron. He was a veterinarian and a big time Saddlebred breeder from Norwalk, a little town south of the city, very close to my uncle's farm which had been sold by now. He was in need of a second groom for a South African rider, in Central Iowa no less. I asked how many horses he had and the response of "one hundred and sixty" was a little unexpected.

Most all of them had descended from one horse still on the property, "Phi-slamma-jamma", the World Champion of champions in the Saddlebred world. Apparently they cloned the little bastards because almost all of them looked just like him and went for as much as one hundred thousand dollars or more a freakin'-piece. I never actually met Mr. Jama but I got the picture.

I'd only be dealing with half of a twenty horse group in training, two and three year-olds., grooming and saddling up to ten a day while the other groom, also a South African, named M.J., would do the other half. Loui, "the greatest

Saddlebred trainer in the world" would ride all twenty, every day, five days a week, and do shows - "sales meets" as Doc Ron called them. And yes, it was Uncle Chuck's Ol' Doc Ron, much older.

Now Saddlebreds were a whole different donkey - tall, skinny and permanently freaked-out looking, inbreds a couple times over, like cousins in the Ozarks. They pranced about like they were walking on hot coals. It wasn't Dressage but some kind of pre-Civil War era bullshit so your buggy would look good going to church on Sunday morning in the Confederate Carolinas. Excuse me, Scarlet, this was an archaic industry, battling the protests of the P.E.T.A. people, yet defiantly "trotting on"... and the only work I could find.

The feeding and mucking was handled by another group of guys. My first task in the morning was to turn out four of my trainees from the north end, then begin saddling from the south. I was also instructed to place four heavy chains made like bracelets, one on each foot, before they were taken out.

I walked the first one out, "Phlame." He picked up his feet like they were stuck in bubble gum, very similar to Casino Nick and the duct tape socks. It occurred to me these horses were having it drilled into their psyche that they had to high-step like Hitler all the time.

The place had the feeling more of a factory than a barn. Mute Mexicans cleaned the stalls ahead of us. Actually there were no Mexicans in Iowa when I grew up. They must have shown up to pick corporate corn.

Rockets on a Rope

Another new first for me were these body harnesses - sadistic straps, buckles, and belts with an aluminum "bucket thingy" that held the tail up all night and all day, except when they were riding. These things were like blankets only they couldn't lie down and it was completely barbaric. I was also told one horse in the line up, "Phorget Me Not", was to have an electric buzzer placed under a lunging harness that Loui could activate as he barked commands.

If she didn't respond, she'd get some encouragement. Now the best part about working for Doc Ron was this: He was a nationally acclaimed vet, and on top of that Reedannland was one of the world's tip-top Saddlebred growers in a predominantly midwest market.

Now the best part about working with a vet around is all the stuff you have around to make the day fun for everyone. If a horse needed it's tail worked on, you "tranquilized" it. When you needed to shave it's feet and/or ears, you tranq'd it. If a horse pissed you off, you tranq'd it. And if you just didn't want to deal with their sorry-ass whining... Well, you get it.

These bastards were being taught to dance like Cossacks real fast and then sold and shipped off. Bring in the next batch of babies. Phi-Slamma-Jama indeed. Assembly line equine products...A.S.A.P. These people should have the P.E.T.A. people peeing their pants and passing out. Some of these "babies" were going for as much as $200,000. I'm thinking to myself some Amish Neanderthal with a buggy has got $200,000 to burn on a jerked-off "Jama" that looks like it's about ready to explode?

The first "big deal" horse on my cell row was "Que Pasa." Just his name made me homesick. On top of and underneath that mid-evil harness holding the tail in place, the horses had actually been surgically altered, snipped under the root of the tail, right above the "poop chute."

I was now being shown by Master Loui, "See here. You dip a finger full of this ginger and then stick it in their butt and swirl it around." Aaahh? Are you serious? I'm serious. This stuff came in a bottle brewed by some hillbilly in Missouri, specifically for the Saddlebred crowd.

As Loui stood there talking with his thumb up Que Pasa's ass, I couldn't help but wonder "Where had I gone tragically wrong?" Was it the affair? The drinking? The music business? Jesus! That was it! I should have never left LA. I would have been better off dying in a fiery plane crash, in a bath tub, in Paris.

As I stood there contemplating how much Bute it would take to kill myself, the horse's tail began to slowly rise like some equine erection that Loui was looking for. "See there. Now that's how it's done," he exclaimed like some queer circus carnie. "Ok. Now saddle him up with the barb wire bit and let's get going, shall we? Bring him to me when he's prepared."

"Yes, Commandant." I clicked my heels. Holy Jesus! This was "Auschwitz for horses." I'm not gonna go into the day to day crap that went on, but I will add at this point: "Phorget Me Not" figured out I was the guard putting the shocker device on and she had developed a strong disliking for me. A first.

My hands were finally starting to wear out after a thousand stall snaps and shovels and saddles and shit. I had started to wrap them in polos I'd poked thumb holes in, leaving my fingers exposed for the ginger trip and tongue-ties that Loui said would keep them from "playing with the barb wire bit." As the Mexican boys loaded the trucks for the first show, I strode into the barn in a pair of snappy white tennis shoes as I didn't need leather work boots because if one of these freaks stepped on your toe, they'd pick up their foot so fast you'd think they thought you were gonna "tranq" em or something. I was also sporting a new fresh smelling long sleeve t-shirt that said "I'm with Stupid" and had an arrow pointing to the right. Loui explained I wasn't wearing that to the show.

Springfield, Illinois looked just like Iowa - one big cornfield with an Interstate running through it. Even the big brick barns at the fairgrounds appeared to be built by the same guys, possibly Amish. After we put the inmates away and the guys finished hanging the banners and buckets, we all went to dinner on Doc Ron where I was informed I'd be rooming with Loui at the masochistic motel, just up the chocolate highway.

We didn't have to be to the barn until 10 a.m. which was not cool. I had always started the day with my charges and ended the show with them. On top of that, sitting that morning watching TV with Loui holding the remote made me really uncomfortable.

As we got in the truck to head to the barn, I threw in my trusty Boy Scout back pack. It was actually my dad's. When we had loaded in the day before, the place was packed. Apparently in the night one of the enemy horses had colic'd, so there was an empty unclean stall right next to our last horse on the row, Phorget Me Not.

I threw my stuff in the mucky stall. She snapped at the bars of the stall wall between us and ran her teeth along the metal. "Nice. I'm sharing a cell with Marilyn Manson." This had been non-stop fun up 'til now and was shaping up to be just more fun. I missed Joanie, almost.

Harlem's Trend was another horse under my keeping. He belonged to Doc Ron's forty year-old sorority daughter, Becky, who couldn't ride to save her own life. But Harlem was descended from another Harlem, who begot some other Harlem, who begot this one with "Phi" tossed in there somehow. Artificially I'd guess. So this Harlem had to win, or be "tranq'd" eternally.

Now his feet were huge, flat, hardly there hooves. Not at all like the solid upright heel of Dressage. Loui was having a hard time figuring out exactly which set of platform inserts would adjust the angle of the shoe to keep the horse from walking all over himself trying to please the Queen.

The farrier had arrived with three or four different degrees of slants that looked a lot like the shoes Chaka Khan wore during the disco craze. So after firmly nailing the first set on, Loui trotted the big horse around the warm-up arena twice. "No. These aren't right."

They pulled those off and re-nailed the next set. "No. No. Not yet." So they ripped those off. By this time there was hardly any place left to nail in the swiss cheese hoof wall.

"Don't worry. We can body putty those holes up," the farrier assured me. Christ! He was one of them. "And you can paint them black," Loui added.

On the way back to the barn I burdened King Loui: "Wasn't that a bit extreme?"

He shouted back at me, "Nothing is too extreme. We're going all the way to the World Championships."

"No," I shot back. "This is the fucking midwest."

"Don't talk back," he demanded.

"Oh, I got chunks of guys like you in my stool, you South African slave trader," I declared.

We had worked out sort of the same professional relationship I had with Phony Joanie. We had a need for each other's individual abilities but we were not amigos.

The first night "kitten" rustled in her stall next to me all night, farting pretty much in my direction and actually peeing on what seemed to be the opposite side of the wall by my pillow. As I removed the cumbersome tail rack and unwrapped her tail, I was greeted by the putrid odor of infection.

Doc Ron wasn't too concerned. I'm sure he'd seen this quite often, considering. So we loaded her up with antibiotics and thoroughly cleansed the wound, which was fun considering the exhaust pipe location.

This was a concern for me because, in addition to the harness and the surgery and the ginger, a groom would also have to "work" the tail muscle, standing directly behind the horse as close as possible in case they kicked, and bend the tail up over their backs and then crank it back and forth for up to twenty minutes before the ride. She didn't like me in the first place though I'd tried to explain I had nothing to do with the shocker. In theory. It made the whole situation look like certain suicide, which didn't sound all that bad for a racehorse name. The pocket that had once held Joanie's phone and sunglasses now contained four hypodermic needles, all identified by different colored electric tape. White was ace the tranquilizer, always handy. Green was Banamine for if the pony even looked uncomfortable. Yellow was an antibiotic - Don't bother ol' Doc Ron if you see or smell something. "Blast it." Black was the "parking brake", Rompun, which left them still standing, but they didn't know it. That morning Loui was in the warm-up barn lunging a young trainee, "Do You Dare." He was lecturing the horse on the significant interpretation of the word "Whoa." I had never said "Whoa." I was more of a "Don't" or "Stop it" kind of guy. I hissed, "Ssss. Leave me alone." More along those lines. Mazarin responded best to a quick "NEIN."

"Dare" had a unique looking lunging apparatus on that day, with an extra rope running from Loui's left hand to a metal loop ring on the bottom of the girth. From there two rope lines, like a marionette puppet, went down to special loops on the back of the front shoes. Clever. Again, this was probably thought up in the Ozarks. The young Colt jogged joyously along as if in a pasture on a lovely spring day. Loui ordered, "Whoa" and then yanked on the extra rope, pulling the started horse's two front feet up into his chest, hitting nose first in the dirt.

Effective. This definitely got the boy's attention. As the dazed youngster struggled back upright, Loui would "request" in a more "phony fake fag nag" pleasing tone, "Trot on...", possibly Amish. He snapped the lunge line as the horse bolted forward, this time with a fixed eye staring right at Loui as he circled two or three more times. "Whoa,"... BAM. After the horse had recovered consciousness, one last time Loui demanded "Whoa" without pulling the gallows and the horse stopped. Dead in his tracks. He stood like he'd hit a brick wall. He stared wide-eyed at his master with a look like "What's next?"

Rockets on a Rope

By the final day of the show, Phorget Me Not, or "Kitten" as she liked to be called, and I had worked out our differences. She could tell I was trying to help her as I'd smooth cool antiseptic cream on the sore spot under her tail before I yanked it back and forth, up and down, for twenty minutes. Ruh-Row. We were late for a date with destiny. Loui had decided we would paint all the horse's feet black so Harlem would look consistent. Oh yeah, sure. That's gonna look glam on this chestnut orange rock star. All of the horses also had hair extensions. Seriously. Four to six foot wigs made from other horses tails. I could've made some money back on Nikitas, dragging in the dirt as they slid him away.

Finally we had to put a foot long colorful braid that hung straight down behind her bridal path, so when the horse held its head uncomfortably and unnaturally high, the braid would be straight up and down with the world in exquisite Saddlebred form.

The bullshit was all done except, oh right, the tongue-tie and the ginger. In that order, for a reason! We scurried off to the grand ball.

"Oh, nice of you two to show up," Loui moaned.

"Yeah, well I was finishing off a six-pack before we came." Loui climbed up the mounting block. I only gave little girls leg ups, but then, Loui was a little girl in a lot of ways. I held the flowing tail off the floor as I ran behind them, trotting up the entry into the Arena. Now this Saddlebred look is just about as hyped up as possible so, as they hit the arena floor, I would throw the extra long tail into the air to the whoops, cheers, and hee-haws of the distinguished crowd.

As the hicks settled down and the routine started, Doc Ron and I walked up into a balcony just over the arena to watch the spectacle and I hung my worn-out hands over the railing.

"I like what you've been doing with her, son," he said. "You're good with them all and I can see it. Now I know this stuff seems kind of barbaric or brutal to you but it's how I make a living and you're helping me out very well indeed. I know you're missing your daughter and you don't want to be here but I just wanted you to know I think you're one of the best horseman and kindest people I've seen around horses. And I appreciate you being here with us and doing a great job. Loui thinks so too. He just won't show it. But he's told me the horses respond to you."

Right then, as they swept around the corner towards us, I clicked a little, something you do to move them forward. Phorget Me Not jumped and looked directly at me. Doc laughed a huge laugh and said, "See what'd I tell you!" then whooped it up as they came around on the last lap. This time Loui was staring right at me like the nut case he was and Doc yelled, "Wrap it up, ride her home." Or to church on Sunday! "She looks great. Finish it off."

All of them won amazingly enough. Do You Dare wasn't really that into it but "responded." Doc Ron was surprised Phorget Me Not got first place and he gave me a wink and handed me a medal that Loui was supposed to receive. Que Pasa qualified for the *World Championships of the Midwest* to be held in the fall in Kentucky, which he did win - and then was sold to an Amish guy, with a buggy and $200,000 dollars. I'm not making this up. Prince Harlem delivered a smashing Second, which for Becky was a first. And lucky for Harlem. I think Doc Ron knew the judges.

So we all lived happily ever after. We went back to training at Reedannland for a month or so when I was told I wouldn't be going to the next show. Loui's option. M.J,, his squirrelly South African sidekick, would go instead. Fine. I would remain at the farm with Mannie, Doc's second in command, and Raul, a nasty older Mexican who had been there for twenty years. There was also a stallion barn we'd have to feed and we'd have keep an eye on the babies out in the pasture, the horses Reedannland was built upon.

Now when the cats are away, the mice will...whatever, and Raul was a rat. One pleasant morning Mannie storms up to me like he's on "crystal meth" - a popular sport in Iowa these days. He accuses me, saying, "Raul says he saw you smoking meth."

"Look you misinformed Mexicano moron, I'm not from here, I don't even know what meth is. I'm from Hollywood, for God's sake. We smoke a lot of pot."

He stood by his claim, calling Doc Ron immediately to explain my crime. M.J. would later tell me in a phone call that he had actually learned a lot from me, including how to handle Loui, and that one of Raul's friends needed work, so I was the sacrificial lamb.

I also spoke later with "Ol' Doc Ron" who assured me he had heard of this "Coup" and he affirmed his belief in my honest labor and abilities, wishing me well on my adventure.

Reedannland

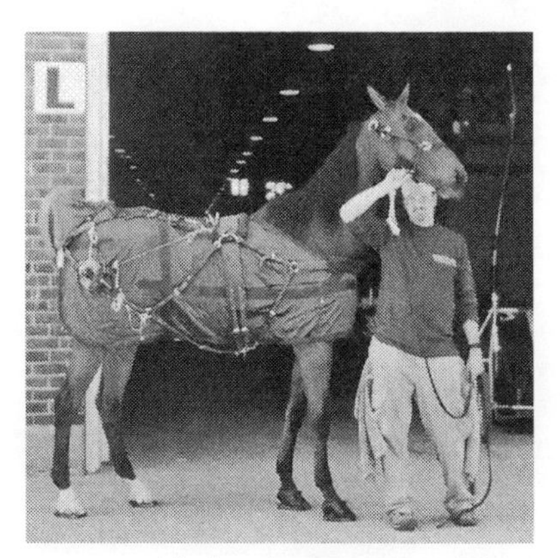

Harlem harness

Neck rigging

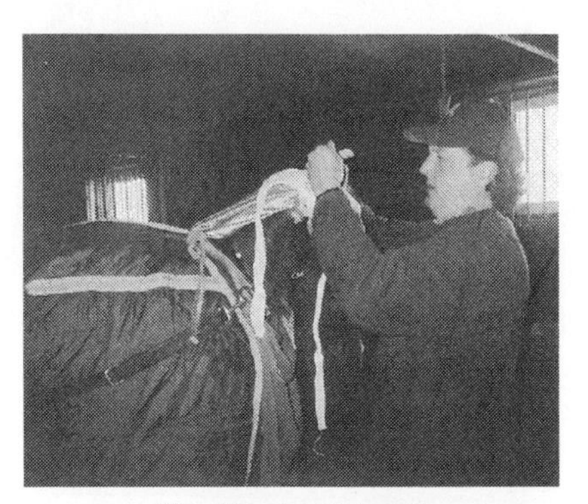

The "bucket thingy"

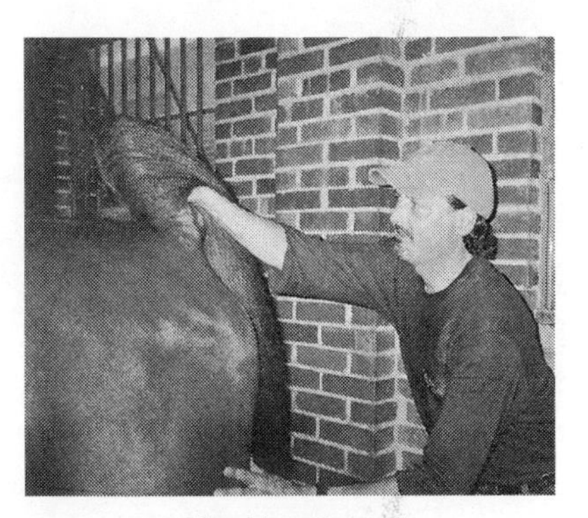

Working the tail

The Saddlebred distinctive trot

Destiny

I had purchased an older Jeep Cherokee with the loot I had managed to save staying with my mom and dad. I stuck around a few more weeks to help around the house, cutting some fire wood with my eighty year-old father and taking the front passenger seat out of the Jeep to turn it into the perfect groom-mobile. I loaded up my belongings and supplies like a puzzle so I could fully stretch out on my own bunk and travel.

I hugged them goodbye and sped out of Iowa at six in the morning for the eighteen hour drive back to my real home. About 6 p.m. I drove through Denver heading south. I figured I could split the drive up and camp out for the night at the Colorado Horse Park in Parker where I had enjoyed my stays previously. This worked out surprisingly well.

As I drove into the facility, a hunter/jumper show was forming. A parade of trucks and trailers were arriving, moving in like an invading army with nice RVs and probably friendly primos. A picture perfect hunter/jumper woman in her late fifties stood frustratingly speaking beside a heap of tack trunks and hay bales. I introduced myself. "Need any help?"

Becky put her phone away as I told her a short summary of my resume. I told her that I was returning to New Mexico with no certain plan and was available now. She immediately hired me and we began arranging trunks in front of stalls and filling shavings, water and hay.

She explained that her wonderful groom, Dario, was dealing with some concerns with his family back in Mexico and that he'd been "a little unreliable as of late." I could fill in for now. She said she'd give me cash tonight and I was to show up at 5 a.m. and see if Dario had returned. I was surprisingly content. She seemed really pretty cool and the horses looked well cared for. When I arrived promptly at 4:45 a.m., Dario was back and there was a stack of clothing - a large black hooded sweatshirt, three black t-shirts and a really cool black fleece vest, all embossed with a dramatic Destiny Ranch design.

"Let's go! Get dressed. Get to work," he smiled, explaining how grateful he was that I had shown up. He was a handsome Mexican, well kept. He offered me a hearty smile and a handshake, explaining how he missed his daughter. She was sick and he wanted to go back to his home for at least a quick visit. So maybe we could all help each other out for a while.

"Thanks for covering me, gringo," he added.

"I'm not a gringo, I'm a primo, primo!" I objected.

He laughed and then got serious for a second, sort of "inwardly". "Come with me, brother. Let's feed the masses."

About 8 a.m. Becky came in driving an SUV. Out stepped her gorgeous trainer daughter, Jamie, and a chubby little thirteen year-old man in expensive riding cloths and a back pack, Marshall. He was an entitled child, from New York City.

He flew out to Colorado in the summers to train and ride with Becky and Jamie. How delightful. He ended up reminding me of a cross between Damanda and the fat kid from *The Little Rascals*. Dario would take care of Jamie's horses and the other students and I was assigned the young gentleman. His two steeds, named Picachoo and Damascus, had flown in a few weeks before for training. He never spoke to me the first few days. I didn't care. I was happy. This was cool. He'd put on his velvet helmet and scurry away after I'd lifted his fat little expensive ass into the saddle.

This was ok for me since I just acted like I didn't speak English. I'd learned this trick in Scottsdale from another handsome Mexican who was actually a marine biologist from Cancun. He just hadn't found his desired position in the promised land yet and realized people asked you to do less stuff if they thought you were stupid. Olé.

Dario had come up with a brilliant plan. After this two week show he'd run down to Mexico and check in with his family and I would fill in at Destiny headquarters.

Becky ran a righteous ranch. Destiny was the immaculate stable with large tack up stalls and huge bathing areas. The impeccable oak wood stall doors had brass latches. The whole place had a synthetic flooring like they used on basketball courts. There was even a viewing lounge on the second floor over the giant indoor arena with candy machines and Mountain Dew you didn't have to pay for.

Jamie was a great rider - beautiful, talented, focused and all her students worshipped and adored her abilities. I figured this must be as good as it gets but I was depressingly aware of my limited engagement and I was only one day's drive from Emily. So I kept it in perspective.

The show went smoothly. Everyone was happy with their success. Marshall had managed to murmur an occasional "Thank you" when I'd hand him a bottled water after the ride. "Fine ride, sir," I would say and he laughed at the things I said to his horses.

When he left the last night, he walked over and politely handed me a crisp hundred dollar bill out of his pants pocket. "Nice job, sir." I wonder if he even knew my name. Becky told me later he'd done that on his own. It was not his father's idea. I liked that. A thirteen year old kid with dinero.

Dario's plans had changed a bit due to some struggles with some documentation problem so he was staying at home base for another two weeks. I told Becky I was fine hanging around the horse park as I'd actually heard a dressage show was blowing in tomorrow. I thought I might be able to catch a ride at that.

The next morning Brian, the show manager, hired me to help his crew clear out the whole facility, five huge barns. We went down the rows, about ten of us primos laughing and singing. We were allowed to drink because it was our one day off weekend. The boys were impressed at how many stalls I was doing per truckload and how clean and neat my row was when we got to it. It was a fun day and it was amazing how the place felt so different without all the white people.

As Luck would have it, an amateur trainer I'd met at Dressage in the Rockies, Joan, drove in with a mid-sized pony that one of her students was supposed to show but the girl had become ill. The horse still needed the qualifying points to proceed on the circuit that summer so Joan was going to ride him.

He was named "Spirit" and the situation was so silly to begin with we both believed it would be funny as hell to have a Jedi groom and we'd pretend the pretty pony was Pegasus. Joan's feet hung pretty far down on the little bugger and we kind of had to rearrange the saddle. But her weight was similar to the fat teenage owner so we just had to punch some holes in the leather straps to make it comfortable. He was actually a talented performer and the other little girls on the grounds knew who he was and who Joanie Bolton was, so we were kind of treated like cosmic royalty. The girls would stroke his mane and offer carrots. "You've moved up to the big time, Spirit." They had no idea.

So I won't have to go over the duties of a groom anymore, I'll just say the show went smoothly and everybody had fun. The weather was great and we pulled in a whooping Third Place finish. When we flipped the judges score card over, on the back written in black magic marker were the words, "Not a good fit." Obviously, the judge wasn't aware of the charming story. Before she drove off, Joan handed me a three hundred dollar tip. I wasn't really planning on charging. "Mucho Bueno."

I drove down about 15 miles south to Destiny Ranch, located in Franktown, for my three weeks in paradise. I secretly wished Dario would get stopped at the border trying to return and spend the rest of his life in Mexico with his family.

I had been enlightened that I wasn't the only dad missing his daughter. It didn't really make it any easier. No such luck. Dario did return, refreshed, and walked up to me boldly. I was greeted by a long, hard hug.

He went right to back to work filling water buckets. It always amazed me that these guys did shows eight or ten months of the year sending most of money home, pretty much living on the show scene, and only saw their family every so often, or not at all. He had a sweet gig and he knew it. It was like living rich without the bullshit. He said, "Hey, stick around with me. We could be a team and go to the Indio show" in the desert of California for a three month show and walk away with $5000 each. I told him he should stick with the Destiny deal and I needed to get home to see my own little girl for Christmas.

Jamie thanked me for my service which I assured her had been a pleasure. She suggested an older German Dressage officer from nearby Castle Rock who was looking for a live-in groom for seven horses. A predicted twenty inch snow storm began to fall that afternoon and for some reason I drove out to the farm. Now I really don't remember his name. It was something like Hess or Himmler. Something charming. I unloaded some of my stuff into a bunk house at the back of the barn in a blinding snow storm and decided to give it a go.

This old man was completely nuts and completely German. Right from the start instead of fluffy wood shavings, he had sand in the stalls! This made no freakin' sense at all! He didn't allow nose chains to control them. Instead he preferred to shake the ropes in their faces and slap them silly.

Rockets on a Rope

He was a total creep.

His feeding charts were bizarre at best. They made no sense. Almost anything I did was met with a loud, "No! ...This is how I do it! You must do as I do - how it should be done - like this!"

I began planning my departure as the first day came to a close. At this point I was snowed in like the Romans. I would have to stick it out a little longer.

Over the next two weeks I would drag the sand and manure mixture out into a large snow-covered pasture on the side of a hill overlooking the small right-wing town. I began spreading it out in a twenty foot straight line square, not attaching the corners.

A few days later after it snowed again, I would spread perpendicular strips, also not connecting them, as the snow continued to cover my artwork. On the day I was ready to go, I informed Adolf I was leaving. I needed to get back to Emily. Then I strategically filled in the remaining sections of my masterpiece...

As I drove out of the ranch driveway I lit a cigarette and smiled. I anticipated the crystal clear spring sunshine and melting snow would reveal a forty foot square horseshit and sand Swastika on the side of the hill above the sleepy hamlet. "Auf wiedersehen. Guttenberg!" I'm pretty sure we won the war.

I drove out to the Colorado Horse Park as it began to snow again. Brian, the facility manager, offered me a job at the full time boarding barn for winter and a chance to work on the crew at the shows starting in the spring.

Destiny

A wonderful opportunity. And it came with a trailer! But after viewing the shelled-out, mice poop-filled, beer can-littered, shoebox in the barrio and then considering my neatly packed jeep containing 3 guitars and all my recording equipment that I still carried with me - as the snow got heavy I chose to head back to Tesuque.

Me and Emily

Last Call to the Vet

Now the best part of writing this book has been that I'm not making any of this up. The timelines have been bent in a few locales as well as there being a few character composites and I'm leaving a ton of stuff out, like I probably messed around with the braiders a bit more than I mentioned. If anybody's going to sue me over this book it would be one of them.

Over a period of years I had been picked up a number of times hitchhiking in Santa Fe by a quirky girl named Elizabeth Wallace. She was a unique thing, just finishing up studying to become a nurse. I drove into Tesuque with no certain plan and bumped into her again at the village market. This time she was on a Buell 1200 Thunderbolt motorcycle. After dinner we returned to her place - for the rest of my life.

There was a new vet in town who had built a fancy state of the art horse hospital out by the movie sets in

Rockets on a Rope

Cerrillos - "Dahl Equine". I applied for a job, frankly a little wore out on this horse business. Reluctantly, on both our parts, I took the position. He had heard a lot about me already through other people, who had repeatedly informed him of my "way" with horses.

He seemed a likable enough fellow, very sure of himself in a shaky rich kid sort of way. He had grown up on a big cattle ranch in the Mora Valley, just east of the Pecos. He had been reared rather well. He knew and cared a lot about horses. He was a great vet. He had built an impressive facility but there was one slight imperfection to this set up. Barb, his wife, a lawyer by nature, had absolutely no clue as to the existence of Equus Cabballus. Nada. Nothing. She was not a horse person. And if she'd like to comment on what I am about to reveal, and receive what I am about to say - and say well, if i do say so myself, which I do - I invite the interest.

From this day henceforth and in addendum, if any of the afore described horses or their attorneys would like to consult me, I shall leave my phone number on the barn blackboard. Don't call if it's only an infection. I present my carrot.

I was about to meet a new horse, "Ketamine" and another bottle of stuff they use to kill horses that said "Stuff they use to kill horses" on the label. These were both kept in a vault under a lab table. The first couple of months I started at the boarding barns on the hospital grounds mucking and feeding twenty private horses. There were other vet techs and doctors and secretaries inside. I was just learning the ropes.

Dr. Thug Dahl started using me a lot to lead a horse, while he studiously watched it trot to observe leg problems, which there were a lot of and he was very knowledgeable about.

He was impressed I could take any horse, in any condition, off a trailer and up the concrete rubber incline into the horrifying chamber of doom.

Getting a horse into the menacing metal stocks, with a two inch fence post hole in their skull and blood covering their eyes, while they were going every which way, sucks. Alas...I was very good at it. Thug tended to yell at me in front of the clients, which also sucked. And it was mostly about methods, not whether I was doing something, but more technically how I was doing it.

He was a firm believer in the sagging 7 inch rope leading method, but after the race track, etc., I had really found out that holding them right on the halter snap ring, right under the chin, and sort of riding them from the ground with your elbow on their shoulder - your legs in line with their front legs - actually worked best. He had a hard time accepting it, but I was better at it than he was. He had thoroughly been whipped into being a disciple of the Ray Hunt method of horsemanship, hunt me up, while I had this sort of Zen like mismatch of things going on that seemed to work a hell of a lot better.

Holding the wiggling horse's head while Thug went shoulder deep into its portal was also an exhilarating experience for me, the horse, the concerned owners and the good doctor. He also did this a hell of a lot, sometimes with an ultra-sound device on pregnant mares. Once we preformed an abortion on a mare with twins. There's so much legs and horse in there already that two tend to not work out. Usually one is deformed or not fully developed or they both die. So, as Dr. Dahl made faces, shoulder deep, about to separate the fetuses, the owner quietly said, "Make sure you leave the fastest, best looking one."

We had an Endoscope we could send up their nose, all the way down to their stomach to see what was going on, if you didn't rip the hell out of the throat on the way down. That was wild. To do this you'd use a twitch, which was an ancient device with a rope loop at the end of a baseball bat. Probably Roman. While I was placing the loop over the horse's lips then spinning the wooden handle, tightening the noose on the nose, I said to a freaked-out client, "Don't worry. It acts like an endorphin, relaxing and numbing them."

"That's a sweet story," Thug laughed. "Actually it just hurts like hell and gets their minds off what we're doing, which hurts more."

I really started to learn a lot about colic and other situations I'd been dealing with for years from the outside. Another duty, when the horse was totally sedated and while Thug doctored some hideous wound on a hind leg on his hands and knees, would be for me to push the looming animal's chest off the front bar of the stocks so he wouldn't suffocate while he was dying of something else.

Babies were really fun too, holding them bent over at the waist, sometimes for quite awhile, unfortunately with your left shoulder on the colts shoulder, bone to bone, your arm gently across his chest like a gate, and your wrist on the other blade with your fingers extended out - not holding while you were holding. Zen Cowboy stuff. Then with your right hand you'd slowly grab the base of the bushy tail. Holding... but not holding. Still able in a split second to lift his back feet off the ground or toss him over into the dirt. This was especially enjoyable with projectile diarrhea, which there was a lot of, especially with the malnourished ones, which there were a lot of.

Rockets on a Rope

Brought in by greasy Mexicans in clean cowboy hats that never looked like they fit and fancy pointy toed clean boots, they explained, "While we have no money, this horse was the son of the son of the son of Cigar and it could work out well for all of us in the end." Sometimes the infants had undeveloped hoofs. They were affectionately known as flipper.

There were dog attacks, snake bites, porcupine quills, bad teeth, ticks in the ears, worms, not enough of this, too much of that, purple piss, puss, and pizza. One night we were working on another hole in the skull, while eating a pepperoni pizza. I think the owners were shocked.

Once a colt came in with its entire face peeled off from ear to ear, forehead to the top of the muzzle, scalped as it were. The hide was hanging off its nose but there was a surprisingly small amount of bleeding. I spent 3 hours holding his sedated head on my shoulder and neck while the doctor performed what basically was plastic surgery. It turns out that something had spooked the baby while he was eating out of some old metal feeder. As he reared up, it just ripped his face off. We went through so much hydrogen peroxide, iodine, water, work, just making complete sure it was completely clean underneath. Amazingly it worked.

A lot of these accidents were often "unexplainable" and always billed to the healthy account of one "Elliot the Idiot". I found out the most obvious answer or reason to why horses got hurt was stupid people - period - and I learned to not trust people.

Now most of Dr. Thug's techniques worked. I just didn't like how he explained things. It was kind of like asking Sarah how to find the stalls in Tucson.

Last Call to the Vet

There was another vet at the hospital, "Berkley", who was a Kentucky trained surgeon with a bedside demeanor and knowledge everyone appreciated and another vet tech in-training, Akara; both whom were a hell of a lot cuter than Thug's wife. Both suddenly up and quit one day, or so I was told. Apparently Thug and the two of them no longer had any need for each another. This increased my vet assist time considerably. And I was still maintaining the boarding barn on weekends.

My first emergency farm call was fifty miles away in Stanley. A woman named Lori, who I'd known for many years, had a mare with a gaping chest wound probably from a barb wire fence. She had given premature birth to a filly in the middle of the night. Laying in the dirt, now dehydrated, she had probably not received the vital first feeding of colostrum.

I was instructed to bring the large box of medical supplies from the truck into the corral where Lori held the upset mare. My job was to lie down on the struggling filly without really laying down and hold her legs - really hold them, while Thug tried to get an I.V. needle into the lightly pulsing hair-thin veins.

He yelled about the kicking, "I'm trying to do something here!" (I think we knew that) as he frantically started a saline solution with electrolytes and God knows what else. This took what seemed like eternity as Lori got distracted from what she was supposed to be doing and the mares stomping feet went four inches past my face into the un-mucked dust. "Pay attention!" Thug yelled, apparently to all of us.

Eventually we got her set up and decided the mare's wound was already drying and dirty, so we'd just load them up and go. I carried the tired foal, as Lori ran along side with the I.V. bag up to Thug, who had already loaded the tranquilized mare.

On the way back to the hospital he explained the colostrum deal was crucial. The I.V. was only providing fluid, no nutrition, and that we'd need to milk the mother when we got back, which they don't like. Time was of the essence.

Now one of Dr Thug's favorite hobbies was putting horses on I.V's for days, weeks sometimes, racking up vet bills in the five thousands. In this case it was extremely needed. In many it was futile and expensive, often done on horses that were only worth two hundred bucks to begin with, who died anyway. This helped out with overhead expenses Barbie pointed out at the weekly office meeting, where we had to sit and listen to her talk about shit she didn't know anything about while Thug stared at X-Rays.

"Boarding doesn't even pay for hay," she formulated. Anybody who's tried to make a living off horses realizes that. Unless you were like Doc Ron and grew your own... hay.

A few weeks later these two did recover and I called Lori at home to say I was glad I got to help and that I wished them well. When Lori mentioned to the doctor how much she appreciated my help and my call, Thug exploded.

"Don't ever call my clients! You're not the doctor. Don't talk to anyone about me."

I wasn't talking about him. Whatever.

My next road trip was to the little village of Galisteo to a place owned by a woman named Pricilla whose family owned a well known bar and Café called The Pink Adobe. She needed routine maintenance checks and vaccines. As we drove in, Thug cautiously asked if I knew her. I suggested, "Probably not."

"Yeah. Well don't talk. Just hold the horses," he said.

"Okee-dokee-pokee. No habla englees."

My shoulder length hair was now whittled down to a balding, gray mess that I kept under my old "Dressage in the Rockies" cap. I had a beard and felt I generally had an anonymous vet tech look going on.

As I held the last horse, Pricilla matter of factly said, "Well, hello Britt Darby."

I looked behind me. Then back at her. "Oh, yeah. Hi Pricilla."

"You two know each other?" the paranoid doctor inquired, popping a few three-hour energy pills.

"Why, yes," she said. "He and Val Kilmer ripped through my bar one night and three of my best waitresses disappeared for two days."

"Wow really? Jeez, I don't recall that," I said vaguely.

On the way back to the hospital Thug sheepishly asked, "Is there anything else I need to know about?" I thought about suggesting *The Tibetan Book of the Dead* or possibly *How to Win Friends and Influence Enemies* or *The Autobiography of a Yogi* ...but I chose otherwise and I obediently responded, "Probably not."

Rockets on a Rope

One of the more interesting cases was an elderly woman with an elderly horse that had a wound on its hock, a place that's hard to heal in the first place. Lots of horses bang them up all the time getting up from laying down. Plus with the age of the horse and constant fussing with medications, leg wraps, antibiotics, homeopathic - they tried this, they tried that - it was not healing. The bill was astronomical!

Finally one day, as we all stood around trying to decide what to do next, Dr. Dahl asked Pedro, an older Mexican who worked in the boarding stables, what would he do. Pedro shook his head sheepishly, knowing full well you never make suggestions in front of a client - in front of the Doctor! But Thug said, "No, go ahead. Tell us. What will cure this horse?'

Pedro said, "My Grandfather would have put sugar on it." So that's what was done. And it worked! Pretty quickly, and the grateful owner slipped an astonished Pedro $250 the next week. He asked me, "por que?" The hospital bill was $2500. For what?

One fine day I participated in my first full-blown surgery - with the cap and gown and rubber gloves and all ...just like *M*A*S*H* - standing by Dr. Dahl, handing scalpel, gauze and three-hour energy pills, as his shaky hands tried to remove three metal pins that had been placed in a young horse's broken knee a few months before. Twenty years ago they would have just shot him. But due to scientific breakthroughs we were digging in.

Now, "Break-a-Leg" Dahl, as I've heard him referred to, was cutting and nervously ripping through the healed skin that had covered the wound, hunting for the shiny pins in the bloody mess, when the horse started groaning and moving. "Your patient is getting ready to leave," Thug yelled at

Last Call to the Vet

Brian the anesthesiologist, a twenty year-old kid from Truth or Consequences, who had probably fallen into the veterinary arts the same way I had, with no formal schooling.

He abruptly cranked the gas up which, when mixed with the Ketamine and God knows what else, produces a state of NOT the tranquil meditative slumber you think Toto's in while she's getting spayed. Actually it is a PCP (angel dust) /LSD like trip to a French restaurant. When they come out of it and you're holding them saying, "That wasn't so bad now, girl," they're actually thinking, "What the fuck was that, Dorothy?"

"I think we're done," I said, pointing to the last of the pins laying on the floor by the doctor's feet. "Don't contaminate the field," he cried, referring to me brushing his sleeve as he continued searching. "All right, lets wrap it up," he said authoritatively. We lifted the heavy body with a sling and a transport that was attached to the ceiling into a rubber walled recovery stall between the O.R. and the office. Barbie burst in, startling the groggy Grateful Dead fan and said, "I need to run into town to get some 'Stay off the grass' signs" as we stood silently watching the horse return to reality.

Later that day Gilly, the hunter/jumper boarding barn trainer, kharmically informed me that Joanie Bolton was trying to reach me. I believe I heard the haunting melody from the movie *Love Story*, you know the one where Ali Macgraw dies in the end. Very depressing.

I gingerly, and I use that word rarely, dialed the number of my favorite ride and struggled with my "inner thoughts" for the next couple of days regarding her latest offer. She had a new barn and the same students. I'd be grooming and saddling, no mucking. Manuel was there. Kind of a nice situation, if it didn't come with so much baggage. And guess what? She had a new four year-old colt - Max ...the son of Mazarin.

I had never forgiven her for Nikita and Maz. I eventually turned her down. We parted as friends. We'd been through a lot together. She still is the best rider I've ever seen ...a true rodeo queen.

I was making a good living risking my life every day and she was only paying eight hundred a month with a small apartment which I didn't need. Liz was now working twelve-hour shifts at the local hospital. My road trip days were over. We had a twenty-nine speed tandem mountain bike we were riding a lot on her days off and I was gaining quite a bit of experience at the vet despite the horror of the whole situation. I innocently told Joanie of a rider in the boarding barn who was good with her horse and had been wanting to move and needed a job. It was a done deal, I was staying at the horse hospital. Or so I thought!

About noon the next day I ran into Thug, who screamed at me, "You're talking to that Bolton woman, person about me. I won't stand for that."

"Well it wasn't really about you," I said.

"I don't care. And one of our boarders is leaving to that Bolton person's place," he spat at me. "That's six hundred dollars a month boarding. That'll cost you."

I wondered what the effects of seven three-hour energy pills would be.

Last Call to the Vet

"Well uhh, I think she was planning on leaving anyway."

Suddenly he turned the other cheek and informed me, "If you're willing to shut up and get back to work - and you really are doing a great job - then I'm willing to accept that." I couldn't figure out where he was going with all this but it seemed like it was going end up something like "And if you just suck my..."

"Barb-wire" burst in with a thirteen-page amendment that read, "You fucked up." I signed it and left. Now oddly enough, earlier that morning I had been rubbing Nitro-glycerin on a horses swollen leg with thin rubber gloves that had torn to pieces as I rubbed the furry bone. I mean, "Nitro." That's what it says on the label and that's what it was.

Liz informed me later that night, "I told you already to wear two pairs of gloves when you were dealing with stuff like that. Are you listening to me? Do you hear?"

"Yeah, sure. I'll have another beer," I said. Now the combination of the alcohol and the nitro were making me a bit giddy and kind of making me feel like I needed to call up Dr. Dahl to let him know how much I had appreciated his employment. That was a fun call and I won't even go into all I said because I'm hoping to sell this book to all the "Pony clubbers" out there and their fathers and their vets. Which, if I was gonna call one, I'd suggest Stuart.

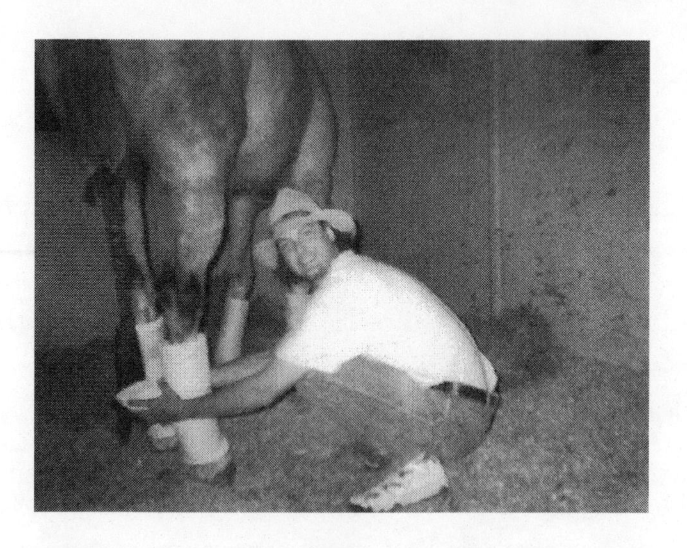

The Cutest Vet in the West

Now I'm going to share three more short stories. The first will warm your toes and the other two will burn them off like you've had your feet too close to the fire for too long. These events happened back when I first lived in Tesuque and I did weekend mucking at the Ark Vet on the days they were closed. I wasn't a tech. I was just there to feed, water and clean up.

One day I was in one of the clinic stalls mucking around an old but well taken care of, worn-out quarterhorse who looked like he'd seen enough days roping and riding.

On a bench next to a tough looking fifteen year-old cowboy, sat Stuart with his elbows on his knees and his hands clasped on his forehead. He looked like he was praying in church or waiting for some inspiration. He explained to this stone-faced kid that "Besides the fact this horse was just plain old and what would have to be done or what they could try to do, would or wouldn't help," this could cost up to as much as five thousand dollars for possibly nothing. The kid said he didn't care.

Rockets on a Rope

“Go ahead. Try...Please!”

”Now Troy, I know this horse has been with you since you were little.”

”Four,” the boy submitted as a tear started down Stuart's cheek.

“And I can take your money. Lord knows I need a new truck. But my advice to you, and you can do whatever you want with it is...get yourself a new horse. Get a five thousand dollar horse, ya know? Just start over. I swear to you, that’s what I’d do.”

I was kneeling next to the horse in the stall as he nibbled on my cowboy hat. Things got quiet.

Before he left that day, Stuart walked over to me, looking kind of puzzled and scratching his head. He asked me, “How’d that horse get over there?" pointing to a filthy horse I’d moved over to an empty pen to make it easier for me to clean.

Stuart looked at me kinda disturbed and drawled, “That nasty little roan is one of those B.L.M. (Bureau of Land Management) mustangs from the mountains over by Las Vegas and we had a hell of a time chasing him into that stall. I don’t think he’s ever had a halter on.”

“Well he has now,” I said. Nobody had explained that to me.

Ok. Now this is where it really gets fun. Just as Stuart was ready to leave again, a beat-up pickup truck with a one-horse trailer rattled up to the gates. On the side read, “Earl Fletcher’s Rodeo Horses, Breeding and Training". Now how exactly you train a rodeo horse is a mystery to me.

But I assume it's exciting. Stuart leaned over to me with his dashing grin and sort of grimaced in a straight line, an expression he had while explaining to a bewildered owner, "Well, he appears to be pretty uncomfortable, in my humble opinion." (Grimace.)

Anyway he leans over and says, "Don't help this son of a bitch. He's nuts. Just stand over here with me." Right then the back door of the trailer flew open and the bucking bronc backed out of the trailer, rearing up and spinning around sideways.

Then he came straight down on one of those green T-fence poles that had a no parking sign on it, stabbing through his belly like a merry-go-round painted pony. As he slid to his knees quivering, three shots from a Colt 45 blew up two feet away from Stuart and me. The horse disintegrated.

"Jesus, Earl! Get the hell out of here!"

We both stared solemnly as blood poured out all over the clean dirt.

"Britt, go get the truck and a chain and get that horse off of there and out into the weeds now, before some woman and her daughter show up."

I turned up the volume on the big vet truck's radio. It was playing Willie Nelson's *Mammas, Don't Let Your Babies Grow Up to Be Cowboys*.

I stepped on the gas and the 4x4 strained, spinning its tires for a few brutal seconds, before it sprang forward on its appointed duty. With a trail of blood in the rear view mirror, I raced out to the field, then went back and hosed the dirt parking lot down.

The Cutest Vet in the West

Last story...I promise. My hands are getting tired. Again it was the end of the day, on our day off. It seems horses are alive all the time. They don't take holidays or days off or vacations, unless you're driving.

I was just finishing up water buckets when Stuart came out with his cell phone and said, "We've got a mystery coming in, right away." A rider had called to say his horse just froze up, paralyzed in the front two legs. They'd had to lift him into the trailer backwards. Stuart had already called a friend at a big vet college who advised, with all the West Nile and bizarre viruses going around, it was best to put the horse down, cut him up, box the brain, heart, liver and lungs with the four legs and at least one eye and FedEx him in Freon, as soon as possible, to the University for testing.

As the trailer rolled up, Stuart came out of the office with a case of beer, a bow saw and some silver buckets.

"You up for this?" he asked, handing me a beer. He'd already had two.

"Sure, sounds...educational."

It was. As the owner drove away and we downed another drink, Stuart slowly injected the strange colored substance into the motionless animal's vein and then the horse kind of teetered, like a wooden rocking horse, and fell over sideways.

He began hacking the legs off like he was cutting firewood as I boxed them up and labeled them with the horses name, "Satin." He then split open the belly as a rush of dark blood flooded the concrete floor. The organs were quickly removed and put in the buckets. He looked up at me and said, "I'm not really sure what it is we're standing in." (It turned out to be Tetanus.) Last but not least he severed the head at a soft spot behind the ears, as I held the still warm muzzle and the back of the skull of the being I was just holding the rope for earlier, guaranteeing him everything would be alright. Then using a surgical saw and chisel he removed the brain and an eye. "I don't think he minds, do you?" Stuart tossed up a bit of humor.

When the FedEx guy showed up and saw we were out of beer and soaked in blood, he reluctantly asked what was in the boxes. "A whole horse," I said, wiggling my toes in my blood soaked socks. On the sides of the boxes Stuart had scribbled the destination, owner's name and the horse's name, "Satin". But it looked like "SATAN" as Stuart had sloppy handwriting that night. Since we were drunk, we blew up some rubber surgical gloves and I stuck them on the side of the skull where the ears went and put on a blood-red sponge nose and hung it up on the wall. It was Christmas Eve...

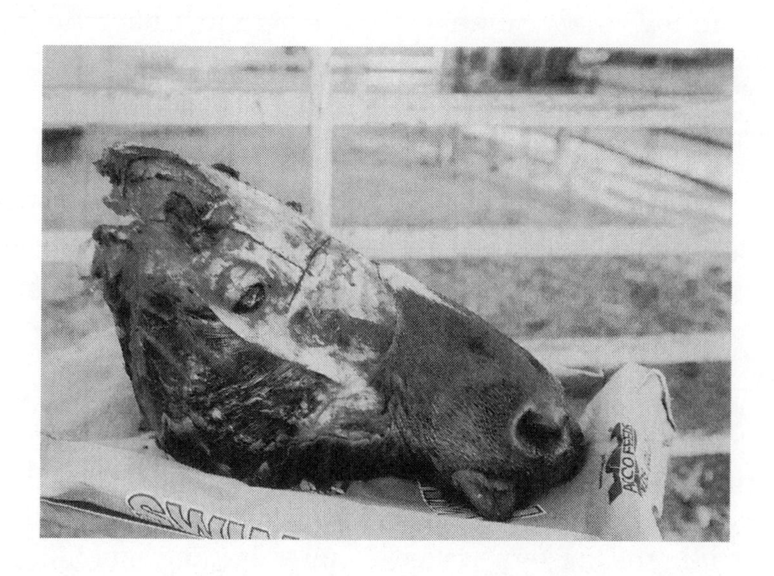

Green Gate Ranch

When I first started this book I thought it was just going to be about horses, but it turned out to be about my whole life and apparently I spent a hell of a lot of time with horses, which I wasn't expecting. I was actually a real musician and lived my life like one in every situation, whether that was a good idea or not. I've been amazed by the people I've ran into and I'll just drop three last names, I promise.

While I was living in Benedict Canyon in Beverly Hills during when we were recording *Inisosion*, I walked down to the Beverly Hills Presbyterian Church figuring my mom would think it was a good idea. I sat down behind an older couple in the back of the sanctuary. When the minister invited everyone to greet their neighbor, Jimmy Stewart turned around, shook my hand, and asked me to sit with him and his wife Gloria, which I did for the next three Sundays. About all he really told me about Hollywood was that it sucked.

Gregory Peck once gave me a ride in his army green '57 Rolls Royce. He had been recording some voice-overs of the *Bible for the Blind* at Rudy Records while I was working with Crosby, Stills & Nash. We ended up drinking whiskey at the Polo Lounge. He might have started my serious drinking. We discussed politics and religion. "Never a good idea," he told me.

I also got on the elevator once at the Beverly Center with Dick Clark and his wife Kari, which was unexpected. I explained to him how I was the greatest existential poet of the bubblegum pop scene, ever. He explained to me that politics and religion didn't belong in the music business. All in all, it wasn't fate or luck or faith or planned. We're all just floating around on a ball of dirt in the middle of "Nowhere" and there are no rules... *It's just the neighborhood you're in.*

If Brett and I would have stayed in Iowa, we probably would have had a better chance. He ended up leaving L..A. with Kate after Val dropped her off on his doorstep. They played the music scene in the Carolinas with Dave Mathews until Brett went through the windshield of a car at 60 mph and woke up back in Des Moines at his mom's mobile home. He will forever be the most talented, drunk, gifted person I ever met. He is now a Dog Behavioral Therapist at an Animal shelter.

Liz and I moved to Taos. Worn out with the "Californication" and "Texasization" of Santa Fe, I pretty much walked away from the high-dollar horse world. And what I thought was just wear and tear on my hands turned out to be a genetic condition called Dupuytrens Contracture. That has left my little fingers curling up and guitarless for the past few years. I gave up my bitterness for our failure in the music biz (sort of). After I could no longer do it the way I wanted, I stop wanting...to do it. And the last thing I want to be is famous - especially for not doing anything.

I always thought the pain was caused by the horse work. It wasn't. Horses don't cause anything. They just react. So when some know-it-all is telling you, "Oh, they don't kick", well that's not for you to decide. In all honesty, they do.

I was at a horse show once and there was a woman in our row with a horse she'd had for 18 years. Raised it from a baby - best friends. One day, while I was tacking my horse up, I heard a loud crashing of buckets and a scream. It turned out something had happened, it seems, while she was doing something behind her horse. No one saw it but she was kicked right between the eyes, crushing her skull, actually leaving one eyeball in the dirt on the aisle floor. She died instantly. Sweet...

Horses aren't motorcycles. They have their own ideas, schedules, purpose and reality. They are telepathic and transcendent. They live in the immediate moment. Hopefully not the past and definitely not in the future. They know what you're thinking, if you know what you're thinking, and doing it properly, as Ariana would say.

Last year I worked on the TV series *Longmire* as a stand-in for a number of main characters. At one shoot at 2 a.m., up the Pecos canyon on a frigid snowy spring night, I was standing-in while they set up lighting, camera angles, etc. for a Horse Vet. I was on my knees beside a horse that was laying down in front of a burning barn, covered with fake blood and smoldering, yet unbelievably still alive? The Director told me to "kneel closer to its head and pet it, stroke its neck or whatever it is Vets do." (?)

Rockets on a Rope

"They wouldn't do this, that's for sure," I offered wanting to stand up and leave, unnoticed by anyone other than a make-up girl shivering nearby who owned a horse. I did 7 episodes then wore out. It was a stupid show made by stupid people and I think I'm done with TV.

A while ago I was called for a "designated extra" role on a one day shoot in Albuquerque, 150 miles away, playing a specific horse trainer in a new film called *50 to 1* about long-shot Kentucky Derby winner, Mine That Bird.

I was seated next to the three main stars, including William Devane, in a scene where their horse's pole position is decided. The luck of the draw, as it were. When their number is called early, they fall all over me as they rush to select the gate position. We shot this 13 times. The same scene over and over. But here's the catch: They did it in 8 hours instead of a normal 12-hour overtime pay day, so after gas, Mountain Dew and cigarettes and the most onscreen close-up shots ever of any film I've worked on, I made $52...$60 went for gas! I think I'm done with movies.

Horses don't like perfume, cowboy hats, insecure people, or guns. Given their "druthers" they like to just stand around and do nothing. They don't seem to mind cigarette smoke.

Ranch hands have Blue Heelers. Dressage girls actually like Jack Russell terrorists. Velvet heads prefer Corgis. Although each and every horse owner believes “they” are unique, they aren't. In fact, after awhile the cliche and predictable patterns of behavior get boring. I'm talking about the owners. I like the horses. At the rodeo... I cheer for the horses.

Green Gate Ranch

Hollywood is like the racetrack. It doesn't matter how fast or talented you are. There's a lot of ugly people who just know how to dress. And in a room full of egos nobody is impressed.

I've seen horses through so many people's opinions. So many different disciplines. So many ill informed approaches. Rumors of people's perceptions of what a horse needs.

Most of all I love the Ritual of feeding a barn-full of horses - the expectation, the instant reward. Knowing each and every recipe for every personality. And speaking of feeding, hay prices are out of control. The drought in the western states, and even a lot of other places in the country, have made hay a premium need item and causing a barrage of free horses being given off by folks who can't afford to feed them anymore. Even the high country grasses are suffering and making next year's outlook grim. Like Slim used to say, "There's no such thing as a free horse."

I've gotten really great at wrapping my own legs - with horse polos! My feet and knees are shot. My back hurts. My hands are trashed permanently from too many hay trucks and three-quarter ton animals crushing me against stall walls. Countless miles of walking fast in wet boots, sleeping wherever and living on cigarettes, Mountain Dew, beer and whiskey. I've basically been "rode hard and put away wet."

This is where Liz comes in. We've been married 4 years and counting. After Liz was worn out on hospital management in Santa Fe and I'd checked out of the Vet, we bought a house in Taos, New Mexico where we'd both always wanted to live. We just hadn't got there until now. Finally in Heaven...

We named it "Green Gate Ranch" after her grandfather's farm in Iowa. That's right, I married a girl from Iowa who introduced me to green vegetables and baths. Not a fashion model from LA, but the most beautiful woman in the world, or at least the Midwest.

So I've spent the past few years writing this book and building a little barn made with wood and stuff I managed to salvage off the old R.C. Gorman estate, a famous dead indian artist.

Anyway, I put up a flyer advertising my abilities and facilities and the first person who answers is some crazy lady with two wild mustangs from Utah. Can she bring them over right now? I say sure, so they show up. And who is driving the truck? Anastasia Fogelberg. I think that's not coincidence. I surrender. It's *Part of the Plan*.

I obviously dedicate this book to Elizabeth Aidan Wallace, who salvaged me from my sin and loves me still, I hope. She has put up with quite a lot, as I am not an "easy keeper" - and she makes pretty damn good breakfast burrito...

Also to my daughter, Emily Grace, who I've missed so much and love eternally. Maybe this book will shed some light into why and where I missed you so much...

And to my Uncle Chuck and Slim Green, for placing in me a knowledge and love and respect for the Horse...

And to my Mom and Dad who would never let me have a horse of my own, because they were too expensive.

Until the next show, Primo, "Happy Trails."

Taos, New Mexico, June 2009.

Rockets on a Rope

Rockets on a Rope

Made in the USA
Charleston, SC
06 March 2015